THE

REFERENCE

SHELF

ATE DUE

CHILDREN IN CRISIS

Edited by ROBIN BROWN

THE REFERENCE SHELF

Volume 66 Number 1

THE H. W. WILSON COMPANY

New York   1994

THE REFERENCE SHELF

The books in this series contain reprints of articles, excerpts from books, and addresses on current issues and social trends in the United States and other countries. There are six separately bound numbers in each volume, all of which are generally published in the same calendar year. One number is a collection of recent speeches; each of the others is devoted to a single subject and gives background information and discussion from various points of view, concluding with a comprehensive bibliography that contains books and pamphlets and abstracts of additional articles on the subject. Books in the series may be purchased individually or on subscription.

Library of Congress Cataloging-in-Publication Data

Children in crisis / edited by Robin Brown.
      p.   cm. — (The Reference shelf ; v. 66, no. 1)
   Includes bibliographical references.
   ISBN 0-8242-0853-6
   1. Children—United States—Social conditions.   2. Family—
United States.   3. Poor children—United States.   4. Child care—
United   States.   I. Brown, Robin, 1961–   .   II. Series.
HQ792.U5C4318   1994
305.23'0973—dc20   94-2779
                                                                          CIP

Cover: Teacher and student aides oversee day-care center.
Photo: AP/Wide World Photos

Printed in the United States of America

CONTENTS

PREFACE

Childhood in America is changing in some unsettling ways. Currently, sixty-one percent of mothers work, up from thirty-nine percent in 1970. Mothers of children under six are the fastest growing segment of the labor force, putting increasing pressure on the child-care industry. Families are struggling to survive in the midst of a major economic dislocation. A decline in wages adjusted for inflation has made two incomes increasingly necessary to maintain the standard of living that in the previous generation was maintained with only a single income. Under pressure in a recession to be more productive, both men and women are also working longer hours (one estimate suggests an increase from 40.6 hours per week in 1973 to 48.8 hours in 1985). The amount of available time parents have to raise their children has been steadily declining.

How is this "time deficit" or "parenting deficit" affecting the nation? Should we be concerned that there are fewer adults available to coach sports teams and participate in parent-teacher associations? Who is looking after the children whose parents are working a fifty-hour work week? Do we set a high enough value on the raising of children as a measure of human accomplishment? Where is the best balance between work and family for both mothers and fathers? In this affluent nation an increasing number of children are growing up below the poverty line. What can we do to improve the quality of life for all American children?

The first section of this compilation examines the changing structure of the family. Today, twenty-five percent of all children live with only one parent, probably their mother, a statistic that is due to both rising divorce rates and the number of children born to single women. The nuclear family seems to have collapsed in a single generation. Some social science research now casts doubt on whether the single-parent family is a viable structure that can result in healthy, productive adults. *Do* children need both parents? With the entry of so many women into the work force, the role of mothers has changed. Has there been a parallel change in the role of fathers?

The second section describes the crisis in the child-care industry. The increasing number of single parents and two-career families has put an enormous burden on child-care providers. The child-care industry works under the burden of low wages and practically non-existent benefits. The resulting 40% turnover rate among child-care workers is particularly damaging to younger children in need of stability. Should parents be willing to pay more for child care? If parents are already paying as much as they can, should government subsidies be introduced on a wider scale? Should a greater number of child-care providers be licensed? Should the government be involved in child care or is it a private issue?

The third section in this compilation deals with the impact of poverty on the lives of children. Twenty percent of Americans under 18 live in poverty. Many do not have adequate health care and some do not have a home to go to. Homelessness among families is a result of the dramatic drop in the availability of low-cost housing that occurred in the 1980s. When poverty is combined with a public assistance structure that pays below subsistence level, it becomes impossible to pay the rent and buy groceries. The collapse of the nuclear family coupled with a community that has failed to protect the most vulnerable members of society forces us to ask, what happens to a child who is growing up in the poverty of today's inner city?

The final fourth section examines a range of possible responses to the impoverishment of our children. There are cultural changes: a renewed support for parents and families of all types. The corporate sector is also involved, hoping to improve the quality of the future work force. Some say that we lack a coherent national policy to protect and nurture the next generation. An activist policy envisions family allowances and child-care subsidies. Should the government be in the child-care business? Can we afford it? Children challenge our hypocrisy. Is there a difference between our vision of the future and the action we take towards obtaining it?

It has been difficult to read some of the following material and not become concerned about the future. What is illustrated in the articles selected for this compilation, and in the bibliography that follows, is that the debate has opened up. We are beginning the long process of a cultural shift that recognizes not only the rights of adults, but the importance of children and their right to grow up in a safe, healthy, and stable environment.

The editor wishes to thank the authors and publishers who kindly granted permission to reprint the material in this collection.

ROBIN BROWN

November 1993

I. THE CHANGING AMERICAN FAMILY

EDITOR'S INTRODUCTION

In May 1992, Vice President Dan Quayle made a speech criticising Candice Bergen's popular television character, Murphy Brown, for having a baby out of wedlock. Commentary from the media ridiculed Quayle for not knowing the difference between the real world and the fictional world of a television situation comedy. However, Quayle's speech also brought to the surface the great concern over the ways that the family structure has changed in a generation. Did Dan Quayle have a point?

The first article in this section, "Private Lives, Public Values," by William J. Doherty, traces the evolution of the family structure. Writing in *Psychology Today*, Doherty labels the current flexible structure as "pluralistic" and finds there is something to be gained from this flexibility if it is fostered by support from the community. Family ethics can be instilled within this structure, not by going backwards toward older, gender-specific roles, but by moving forward and emphasizing commitment, care, community, equality and diversity in both society and within the pluralistic family.

The second article, "Dan Quayle Was Right," reprinted from *The Atlantic*, examines the cultural trends that have led to this new family structure and the effects this structure has on children. The author, Barbara Dafoe Whitehead, uncovers the fallacy behind the assumption that children will not be permanently damaged by divorce. Divorce carries with it educational, psychological and financial effects that children may experience throughout their adolescent and adult lives.

The third article in this section, "Bringing Up Father," from *Time*, provides a picture of a role in transition. Fathers have received the bulk of the bad publicity in the family-structure debate. The popular press portrays them as absent villains, unwilling to pay child support. Fathers in the 1990s, even when present in intact families, are struggling with the definition of their role, and their chance to make a unique contribution without being cast as "Mr. Mom."

The fourth article in this section, "Endangered Family," looks at the changes in the family structure of the African-American community. There has been a dramatic increase in the number of births to single black mothers. The acts of child-bearing and marriage have been separated. The economic dislocation of the African-American male has led to a whole generation of fatherless children. Leaders in the African-American community are beginning to see this trend as one possible source of the rising crime rates and increasing dependence on welfare rolls. What steps can a community take to heal itself and stop the perpetuation of an underclass?

PRIVATE LIVES, PUBLIC VALUES[1]

Settling down after two decades of tumultuous change, families are painfully caught between their own needs and an indifferent culture. What could help everyone is a dose of reality—a new marriage of family values and public policy.

Whoever said that death and taxes are the only inevitable things in life was overlooking an obvious third one: family. No other social institution surrounds us more intimately from cradle to grave, so shapes our bodies and minds, remains such an emotional presence wherever we go, and gives us such generous measures of joy and frustration. Pretending that family is not important in our lives is like trying to cheat death: it doesn't work and you end up feeling foolish for trying.

Because the family is so central to human life, no one can be neutral about its future prospects. In fact, Americans have been wringing their hands about the state of the family for well over 100 years—with remarkably little change in the tenor of the worries. In the late 19th century, Americans began to focus on the changes wrought by urbanization and industrialization: smaller families, increased divorce rate, less connection to traditional kin and community networks, more child abuse and neglect, and squalid living conditions in urban slums. Sound familiar?

Faced with such changes in the American family, 19th-century

[1]Article by William J. Doherty. From *Psychology Today* 25(3):32–37+ My/Je '92. Copyright © 1992 by Sussex Publishers, Inc. Reprinted with permission.

professionals and community leaders divided into two groups, whose descendants are with us still. The "pessimists" believe that the American family is declining alarmingly in its ability to carry out its functions of child-rearing and providing stability for adult life. The pessimists see the divorce rate—nine times higher than a century ago—as a key indicator of the deterioration of family bonds and the fragmentation of American society. They call for a return to the traditional values of commitment and responsibility, and are appalled by the proliferation of family types and forms in the late 20th century—never-married mothers, single-parent families, step-families, cohabiting couples, and gay and lesbian families.

The "optimists," on the other hand, view the family as an institution that is not declining, but rather showing its flexibility and resilience. The optimists believe that traditional family structures are no longer appropriate for the modern age, and that these structures were too male-dominated and conformity-oriented to begin with. Contemporary families may be less stable in the traditional sense, but most people are still committed to being in a family. It's just that they need a larger menu of family arrangements to choose from. The world is now more oriented to individual options, particularly for women, and the family has changed accordingly. From this point of view, the main problems faced by contemporary families can be traced to the failure of society to accept that the "Leave It to Beaver" family is a dinosaur, and to provide adequate support for the variety of post-Beaver families that now dominate the landscape.

Depending on whether you are in the optimist or pessimist camp, the next decade or two of family life will bring either: a) more deterioration, unless a shift in values occurs; or b) continued creative change, troublesome only if other social institutions keep facing backwards instead of forwards. There is, however, a third orientation emerging, a both/and approach, and I believe it will become more influential in our national discourse about family life in the next decade. This orientation agrees with the pessimists that the family is in trouble and that a transformation of values is needed. It also agrees with the optimists that changes in family structures are inevitable and here to stay, and that both old and new family forms should receive more community support.

We are at the threshold of a new dialogue about family life in the United States, one that transcends the tired debates of the past and that might lead to a workable consensus for the first time in our history. To understand this emerging consensus on the American family, let's take a quick tour of the revolution in family forms in the 20th century.

From Responsibility to Satisfaction

In a breathtaking period of change, the 20th century has witnessed the demise of one standard of family life, the birth of a second, its subsequent decline, and the emergence of a third standard—one that we are still learning to live with. The first two decades of the century were dominated by the Institutional Family as the ideal. The Institutional Family represented the age old-tradition of a family organized around economic production, kinship network, community connections, the father's authority, and marriage as a functional partnership rather than a romantic relationship. Family tradition, loyalty, and solidarity were more important than individual goals and romantic interest. For the Institutional Family, the chief value was RESPONSIBILITY.

The Institutional Family was doomed by the spirit of individualism that developed gradually in the Western world since the Renaissance, and that was given a definitive boost by the breakup of rural communities in the 19th century and the emergence of the modern state. The modern world is based more on individual responsibility and achievement than on traditional family land holdings and kinship connections. In the culture of individualism, as Robert Bellah and his colleagues observed in their book, *Habits of the Heart* (University of California Press: 1985); relationships are based on "contracts"—what people can do for each other, rather than on traditional "covenants":—virtually unbreakable commitments based on loyalty and responsibility.

In the 1970 movie *Lovers and Other Strangers,* a young man, Tony, tells his traditional Italian father than he and his wife are divorcing because "we don't love each other any more." The befuddled father asks, "Tony, what's the story?" For the next several minutes, Tony keeps repeating his explanation, and his father keeps asking, "But, Tony, what's the story?" To a man from an Institutional Family, Tony's explanation did not compute as a reason to break up a family. The scene captured the generational shift from one type of family standard to another.

During the first half of this century, the Institutional Family gave way to the Psychological Family. In the 1920s, family sociologists began to write about the shift from "institutional marriage" to "component marriage." The Psychological Family was a more private affair than its predecessor—more nuclear, more mobile, less tied to extended-kin networks and the broader community. It aspired to something unprecedented in human history: a family based on the personal satisfaction and fulfillment of its individual members in a nuclear, two-parent arrangement.

Marriage was to be based on continued friendship, love, and attraction, not on economic necessity or the requirements of child rearing. Parents were to nurture their children's personalities, not just socialize them as good citizens. The Psychological Family arose during the time when the media and consumerism provided strong competition for traditional family values. If the chief value of the Institutional Family was RESPONSIBILITY, the chief value of the Psychological Family was SATISFACTION.

Nimble for the 90s

Within the Psychological Family lay the seeds of its own demise, as Judith Stacey points out in *Brave New Families* (Basic Books: 1990). Although the ideal Psychological Family was a mutually satisfying, intact, nuclear family, the underlying gender and generational politics were still traditional: male prerogatives were assumed, and the younger generation was to respect the authority of the older.

When the social changes in the 1960s challenged the Psychological Family under the banners of gender equality and personal freedom, the Psychological Family began to give way as a normative ideal in American society. Women began to achieve more independence through paid employment, the sexual revolution made marriage less necessary for sexual fulfillment, adolescents and young adults saw themselves as deserving more and owing less to their families, and men and women alike began opting out of their unhappy marriages in unprecedented numbers. By the late 1980s, the Psychological Family, itself a radical shift from the Institutional Family, had given way to its successor, the Pluralistic Family.

The Pluralistic Family (sometimes called the Postmodern Family) has not broadly accepted an ideal family form. No new single family arrangement has replaced the Psychological nuclear family: instead, a plethora of family types has emerged, including dual-career families, never-married families, post-divorce families, step-families, and gay and lesbian families. Legislative bodies

and courts are beginning to codify the Pluralistic Family by re-
defining the term to include arrangements considered deviant,
non-family forms in the past. Tolerance and diversity, rather than
a single family ideal, characterize the Pluralistic Family.

The chaotic proliferation of family types brought about by
the disintegration of the Psychological Family has stabilized now
around a variety of forms that individuals move in and out of
during their lives. In the Pluralistic Family of the immediate future, an average child can expect to grow up in some combination
of: a one-parent family, a two-parent family, or a step-family, and
will go on in adulthood to cohabitate, marry, divorce, remarry,
and perhaps redivorce.

The Pluralistic Family by definition will have room for some
lingering Institutional Families, and a larger number of nuclear
families representing the Psychological Family. Family forms do
not arrive and evaporate overnight; they just become more or less
normative over time. In the late 20th century, the Psychological
Family hasn't died; it has just become one family type among
others. The chief value—satisfaction—continues to be prominent in the Pluralistic Family, but it is now supplemented by a new
family value for the postmodern age—FLEXIBILITY.

Living with Ambivalence

The near future of the American family lies with the Pluralistic Family. At its best, this completes a century-long trek toward
liberation of the individual, particularly women and children,
from the oppressive features of the traditional family. The Pluralistic Family offers individuals freedom to create the family
forms that fit their changing needs over life's course, with little
stigma about failing to conform to a single family structure and
value system. And it fits the free-form American social life of the
late 20th century, where the pace of life requires quick adjust-
ments and where respect for diversity is a paramount civic virtue.

At its worst, however, the Pluralistic Family is filled with more
internal contradictions and ambivalence than were the Institutional Family and the Psychological Family in their heyday. Surveys indicate that most Americans still believe in the traditional
family values of responsibility and commitment, and most believe
that the stable, two-parent family is the best environment for
raising children.

Family sociologist Dennis Orthner makes a distinction between family "values" and family "norms." He notes that the traditional family values, or ideals, have not changed much, according to national surveys, but that norms, or expectations, for actual behavior have changed remarkably. The discrepancy between ideals for stability and permanent commitment, and the reality of instability and provisional commitment, is one of two Achilles heels of the Pluralistic Family. Most Americans simply do not believe that the Pluralistic Family is stable and secure enough, especially for meeting the needs of children: they feel that divorce and other changes that liberate adults do not benefit their children.

The other Achilles heel of the Pluralistic Family is the lack of support from social institutions. The powerful decision-makers in America tend to be men who were raised during the transition from the Institutional Family to the Psychological Family and who have lived their adult lives in gender-stereotyped, conformity-oriented Psychological Families. They believe in a "natural" split between the private world of the family and the public world of society—although such a split did not exist until the Institutional Family began to break down in the late 19th century.

When the umbilical cord connecting the family and the community is severed, both the family and the community become malnourished. Struggling families are left to their own devices. Family violence is seen as a personal failure, not a social and political problem. And the community loses its sense of moral obligation to promote and protect the welfare of children and other vulnerable citizens.

Accepting the Change

Many business and political leaders are suspicious of the Pluralistic Family, and fear that offering it economic and legal support is tantamount to undermining the American family as they know it—which, of course, is true. On the other hand, as they go through their own divorces and remarriages, and as they see the diversity of their children's families, these men are showing signs of accepting the reality of the Pluralistic Family.

In one sense, the next two decades for the American family are relatively easy to forecast: The Pluralistic Family will be the prevailing norm—and practically nobody will be happy about it. Conservatives will lament the decline of the nuclear Psychological Family, and liberals will decry the lack of community support for alternative family forms. And families will struggle to catch their collective breath following the tumultuous changes of the 1970s and '80s.

As they do so, there is palpable reappraisal about what the family revolution has wrought. The divorce rate has stabilized, and there is evidence that the divorce rate after remarriage is declining. There is growing alarm that the sexual revolution has brought unacceptably high levels of sexual activity among teenagers with an increasing rate of teenage childbirth and a surge of single-parent families. A spate of new books, including Michele Weiner-Davis's *Divorce Busters* (Simon & Schuster; 1992), reflect a popular sentiment that marriage bonds need strengthening—in contrast to books on "creative divorce" of 25 years ago. And bestsellers such as Judith Wallerstein's *Second Chances* (Tichnor & Fields; 1989) tap many Americans' fears that divorce is ruining the lives of our children.

If most Americans are fearful about the family of the future, how have our political leaders responded? They generally don the century-old roles of pessimists and optimists. Pessimistic conservatives decry the lack of traditional family values and call for a values revolution. Optimistic liberals endorse flexibility in family arrangements and call for new government programs. As Daniel Patrick Moynihan noted in his book, *Family and Nation* (Harvard University Press; 1985), conservatives, fearing government interference, like to talk about family values, but not public policies. Liberals, fearing "blaming the victim," like to talk about public policies, but not family values. When it comes to family issues, then, conservatives talk and liberals tinker.

There are signs that we are beginning to transcend this split, accepting the need for change in both private values and public policy. Donald Fraser, the liberal mayor of Minneapolis, an innovator in family support policies, told President Bush [in 1992] that family breakdown is the leading cause of juvenile crime in our cities, a view that Bush repeated in his State of the Union speech. Black columnist William Raspberry regularly decries the deterioration of the African-American family in America, particularly the absence of black fathers from their children's lives, and says that this condition cannot be blamed completely on racism and economic conditions. Jesse Jackson has begun calling for a moral revolution in the African-American community and in the wider society, in addition to more family support from community institutions. Liberals, then, are beginning to talk about values, although conservatives still seem to be slower to talk about policies.

Critics of this recent trend toward emphasizing family values view it as part of a conservative backlash against women's new-found freedoms and acceptance of alternative family lifestyles. For them, the battlefront for families lies only in the public arena, and the emergence of the "V" word (values) is a rear-guard action that threatens needed social change under the camouflage of conservative rhetoric.

Regardless of the merits of these criticisms, family values will clearly be on the national agenda in the next decade or two, as will family-policy issues such as parental leave, child-care, divorce, and child-support laws, and support for families to provide health care for frail members. I predict that the two will become inextricably linked in the future. Family policies will make sense to most Americans only when they are couched in terms of family values such as commitment and care. And espousing values without addressing the policy agenda for families will be seen as posturing rather than helping. What we are approaching, for the first time in our history, is a public discussion about a family ethic to go hand in hand with a family policy.

Emerging Family Ethics

The outline of this new family ethic underlying family policy is beginning to emerge. A new family ethic for the next decade, I believe, will embrace several timeless values of the Institutional Family and the Psychological Family—but go beyond these to incorporate the newer values of the Pluralistic Family. Here are the elements in such an old and new family ethic that I see emerging in the next decade or two:

•*Commitment*—the sense of "covenant" that binds spouses to each other, parents to children and children to parents, and extended family members to one another. Without turning the clock back to an Institutional Family–era when marriage until death was sometimes psychologically deadly to trapped spouses, there will be a renewed emphasis on finding ways to renew troubled marriages rather than end them, especially when children are involved. After a divorce, there will be stronger expectations that both parents remain faithful to the unbreakable covenant that binds parents to their children.

•*Care*—the physical and emotional support of spouses and family members for one another. As philosopher Nel Neddings writes in her book, *Caring: A Feminine Approach to Ethics and Moral Education* (University of California Press; 1984), care builds on

the sense of commitment and requires the ability to empathet-
ically understand one another. To the Institutional Family's emphasis on physical and moral care of children, the Psychological
Family added the idea that parents should understand and foster
the emotional lives of their children, and that spouses should
nurture each other emotionally. These values are relatively new in
human history and will require support from larger efforts for
family-life education in the coming decades.

•*Community*—the importance of the family's ties with its neighborhood, local community, state, nation, and world, with responsibilities going both ways—the family to the community and the
community to the family. This value reflects efforts to mend the
split between the private world of the family and the public world
of the community and its institutions. I believe that community
leaders will increasingly see that the family can be no healthier
than its community—and that communities can be no healthier
than their families.

•*Equality*—the belief that women and men should have equal
say in family matters and should stand as equals in the larger
community, and that children should be given influence commen-
surate with their age and developmental abilities. This is the lit-
mus test for the use of the new emphasis on family values. Will
they become part of an effort to reverse women's gains towards
equality with men, or will they instead become a vehicle for creat-
ing something entirely new in human history—namely, a family
arrangement that provides commitment, care, and community
support within the context of full personhood for men and wom-
en. Ultimately, such equality can be achieved only if it is embraced
at both family and community levels at the same time.

•*Diversity*—the support for all family forms that embrace the
values stated above and provide for the well-being of their members. This is the chief new value underlying the Pluralistic Family,
and I see no way to build a new consensus on family values without incorporating the value of diversity. Such family forms as the
never-married mother with children and gay and lesbian families
are here to stay in a world that accepts the rights of citizens to
form nontraditional family arrangements. This does not mean,
however, that anything goes; all family forms should be judged by
how well they provide commitment, care, and community for
their members. Family arrangements that pass this test deserve
greater measures of community support in the future.

This emerging family ethic is not a recipe for making complex decisions, such as whether to divorce one's spouse. But it does offer guidelines for responsible, caring, and fair actions when individuals are experiencing a problem such as severe marital distress. It also points the way for communities to support these family values with programs and policies.

Here's how this new family ethic could be applied: It could be considered irresponsible to get a divorce without consulting a marital therapist, especially when there are children involved, just as it is considered irresponsible to let someone die without consulting a physician. Communities, for their part, would ensure that marital-therapy services are available and affordable for couples, and just as important, provide funds for community-based family-life education so that more couples will be equipped to handle the rigors of contemporary marriage.

For families going through the divorce process, the new family ethic would expect parents to put their children's interests and needs first, to treat their ex-spouse fairly, and to support each other as parents. Adults would be expected to act maturely and responsibly for the welfare of their children after a divorce, including providing ongoing financial and emotional support. And the community would back these values by offering mediation services, family therapy, support groups, and a non-adversarial legal process.

In the new family ethic, these "shoulds" about post-divorce families would not be seen just as matters of private values and morality—or as nosegays spouted by public officials. They would be matters of major importance to the community. Fathers who abandon their children financially or emotionally after divorce would be subjected to the same social stigma as drunk drivers. The same would go for mothers who try to break their children's bonds with their fathers. And appropriate laws and policies would provide sanctions against these abuses of family values.

At the level of broad government policies, the best way for the government to support the new family ethic is to ensure adequate living standards for families. Almost all serious family problems are more common when income is lacking. In the lowest-income groups in our cities, marriage itself is threatened as an institution, since the majority of births are to single mothers, and the great majority of couples who do marry eventually divorce. In the face of decades of poverty and terrible living conditions, the values of commitment, care, community, and equality are nearly impossible to sustain. That is why calling for a transformation in family values without an accompanying transformation in public policies is like criticizing people for stumbling in the dark instead of offering them candles.

To echo the line from *Death of a Salesman,* most people agree that if the family is to be viable in the coming decades, "attention must be paid." There is little new about the concerns for families, but there are promising signs that we might be able to move beyond the stalemate between liberals and conservatives, that we might transcend the split between the private world of the family and the public world of the community.

This is a perfect time for discussion about a new family ethic, because the wave of changes in the family has subsided for the present. During the years of turbulence, we gained a lot of knowledge from research on families. We now know what factors contribute to better (and worse) adjustment for children after divorce. We now know much more about how to provide educational, therapeutic, and mediation services to families. Marriage and family therapy, for example, has matured in the past two decades as a mental-health service and professional specialty. We have learned that value-free public policies do not achieve a broad national consensus. We have learned that both the pessimists and the optimists make good points, but that the tedious terms of the century-long debate about the American family must be set aside.

The Pluralistic Family is here to stay for an indefinite future. The forces of gender equality, diversity, and personal freedom may never again permit a single ideal family structure like the Institutional Family or the Psychological Family. The quality of the Pluralistic Family of the future depends, however, on whether we can create a new kind of family ethic that will help establish and maintain healthy bonds between family members in different living arrangements, and between families and their communities. Like death and taxes, some kind of family may be inevitable in human life, but the responsible, satisfying, and flexible family required for the next century—that is far from inevitable.

DAN QUAYLE WAS RIGHT[2]

Divorce and out-of-wedlock childbirth are transforming the lives of American children. In the postwar generation more than 80 percent of children grew up in a family with two biological parents who were married to each other. By 1980 only 50 percent could expect to spend their entire childhood in an intact family. If current trends continue, less than half of all children born today will live continuously with their own mother and father throughout childhood. Most American children will spend several years in a single-mother family. Some will eventually live in stepparent families, but because stepfamilies are more likely to break up than intact (by which I mean two-biological-parent) families, an increasing number of children will experience family breakup two or even three times during childhood.

According to a growing body of social-scientific evidence, children in families disrupted by divorce and out-of-wedlock birth do worse than children in intact families on several measures of well-being. Children in single-parent families are six times as likely to be poor. They are also likely to stay poor longer. Twenty-two percent of children in one-parent families will experience poverty during childhood for seven years or more, as compared with only two percent of children in two-parent families. A 1988 survey by the National Center for Health Statistics found that children in single-parent families are two to three times as likely as children in two-parent families to have emotional and behavioral problems. They are also more likely to drop out of high school, to get pregnant as teenagers, to abuse drugs, and to be in trouble with the law. Compared with children in intact families, children from disrupted families are at a much higher risk for physical or sexual abuse.

Contrary to popular belief, many children do not "bounce back" after divorce or remarriage. Difficulties that are associated with family breakup often persist into adulthood. Children who grow up in single-parent or stepparent families are less successful as adults, particularly in the two domains of life—love and

[2]Article by Barbara Dafoe Whitehead. From *The Atlantic* 271(4):47–84 Ap '93. Copyright © 1992 by Barbara Dafoe Whitehead. Reprinted with permission of the author.

work—that are most essential to happiness. Needless to say, not
all children experience such negative effects. However, research
shows that many children from disrupted families have a harder
time achieving intimacy in a relationship, forming a stable marriage, or even holding a steady job.

Despite this growing body of evidence, it is nearly impossible
to discuss changes in family structure without provoking angry
protest. Many people see the discussion as no more than an attack
on struggling single mothers and their children: Why blame single mothers when they are doing the very best they can? After all,
the decision to end a marriage or a relationship is wrenching, and
few parents are indifferent to the painful burden this decision
imposes on their children. Many take the perilous step toward
single parenthood as a last resort, after their best efforts to hold a
marriage together have failed. Consequently, it can seem particularly cruel and unfeeling to remind parents of the hardships
their children might suffer as a result of family breakup. Other
people believe that the dramatic changes in family structure,
though regrettable, are impossible to reverse. Family breakup is
an inevitable feature of American life, and anyone who thinks
otherwise is indulging in nostalgia or trying to turn back the
clock. Since these new family forms are here to stay, the reasoning
goes, we must accord respect to single parents, not criticize them.
Typical is the view expressed by a Brooklyn woman in a recent
letter to *The New York Times:* "Let's stop moralizing or blaming
single parents and unwed mothers, and give them the respect
they have earned and the support they deserve."

Such views are not to be dismissed. Indeed, they help to explain why family structure is such an explosive issue for Americans. The debate about it is not simply about the social-scientific
evidence, although that is surely an important part of the discussion. It is also a debate over deeply held and often conflicting
values. How do we begin to reconcile our long-standing belief in
equality and diversity with an impressive body of evidence that
suggests that not all family structures produce equal outcomes for
children? How can we square traditional notions of public support for dependent women and children with a belief in women's
right to pursue autonomy and independence in childbearing and
child-rearing? How do we uphold the freedom of adults to pursue individual happiness in their private relationships and at the
same time respond to the needs of children for stability, security,
and permanence in their family lives? What do we do when the

interests of adults and children conflict? These are the difficult issues at stake in the debate over family structure.

In the past these issues have turned out to be too difficult and too politically risky for debate. In the mid-1960s Daniel Patrick Moynihan, then an assistant secretary of labor, was denounced as a racist for calling attention to the relationship between the prevalence of black single-mother families and the lower socioeconomic standing of black children. For nearly twenty years the policy and research communities backed away from the entire issue. In 1980 the Carter Administration convened a historic White House Conference on Families, designed to address the growing problems of children and families in America. The result was a prolonged, publicly subsidized quarrel over the definition of "family." No president since has tried to hold a national family conference. Last year, at a time when the rate of out-of-wedlock births had reached a historic high, Vice President Dan Quayle was ridiculed for criticizing Murphy Brown. In short, every time the issue of family structure has been raised, the response has been first controversy, then retreat, and finally silence.

Yet it is also risky to ignore the issue of changing family structure. In recent years the problems associated with family disruption have grown. Overall child well-being has declined, despite a decrease in the number of children per family, an increase in the educational level of parents, and historically high levels of public spending. After dropping in the 1960s and 1970s, the proportion of children in poverty has increased dramatically, from 15 percent in 1970 to 20 percent in 1990, while the percentage of adult Americans in poverty has remained roughly constant. The teen suicide rate has more than tripled. Juvenile crime has increased and become more violent. School performance has continued to decline. There are no signs that these trends are about to reverse themselves.

If we fail to come to terms with the relationship between family structure and declining child well-being, then it will be increasingly difficult to improve children's life prospects, no matter how many new programs the federal government funds. Nor will we be able to make progress in bettering school performance or reducing crime or improving the quality of the nation's future work force—all domestic problems closely connected to family breakup. Worse, we may contribute to the problem by pursuing policies that actually increase family instability and breakup.

From Death to Divorce

Across time and across cultures, family disruption has been
regarded as an event that threatens a child's well-being and even
survival. This view is rooted in a fundamental biological fact:
unlike the young of almost any other species, the human child is
born in an abjectly helpless and immature state. Years of nurture
and protection are needed before the child can achieve physical
independence. Similarly, it takes years of interaction with at least
one but ideally two or more adults for a child to develop into a
socially competent adult. Children raised in virtual isolation from
human beings, though physically intact, display few recognizably
human behaviors. The social arrangement that has proved most
successful in ensuring the physical survival and promoting the
social development of the child is the family unit of the biological
mother and father. Consequently, any event that permanently
denies a child the presence and protection of a parent jeopardizes
the life of the child.

The classic form of family disruption is the death of a parent.
Throughout history this has been one of the risks of childhood.
Mothers frequently died in childbirth, and it was not unusual for
both parents to die before the child was grown. As recently as the
early decades of this century children commonly suffered the
death of at least one parent. Almost a quarter of the children
born in this country in 1900 lost one parent by the time they were
fifteen years old. Many of these children lived with their widowed
parent, often in a household with other close relatives. Others
grew up in orphanages and foster homes.

The meaning of parental death, as it has been transmitted
over time and faithfully recorded in world literature and lore, is
unambiguous and essentially unchanging. It is universally regarded as an untimely and tragic event. Death permanently sev-
ers the parent-child bond, disrupting forever one of the child's
earliest and deepest human attachments. It also deprives a child
of the presence and protection of an adult who has a biological
stake in, as well as an emotional commitment to, the child's survival and well-being. In short, the death of a parent is the most
extreme and severe loss a child can suffer.

Because a child is so vulnerable in a parent's absence, there
has been a common cultural response to the death of a parent; an
outpouring of support from family, friends, and strangers alike.
The surviving parent and child are united in their grief as well as

their loss. Relatives and friends share in the loss and provide valuable emotional and financial assistance to the bereaved family. Other members of the community show sympathy for the child, and public assistance is available for those who need it. This cultural understanding of parental death has formed the basis for a tradition of public support to widows and their children. Indeed, as recently as the beginning of this century widows were the only mothers eligible for pensions in many states, and today widows with children receive more-generous welfare benefits from Survivors Insurance than do other single mothers with children who depend on Aid to Families With Dependent Children.

It has taken thousands upon thousands of years to reduce the threat of parental death. Not until the middle of the twentieth century did parental death cease to be a commonplace event for children in the United States. By then advances in medicine had dramatically reduced mortality rates for men and women.

At the same time, other forms of family disruption—separation, divorce, out-of-wedlock birth—were held in check by powerful religious, social, and legal sanctions. Divorce was widely regarded both as a deviant behavior, especially threatening to mothers and children, and as a personal lapse: "Divorce is the public acknowledgment of failure," a 1940s sociology textbook noted. Out-of-wedlock birth was stigmatized, and stigmatization is a powerful means of regulating behavior, as any smoker or overeater will testify. Sanctions against nonmarital childbirth discouraged behavior that hurt children and exacted compensatory behavior that helped them. Shotgun marriages and adoption, two common responses to nonmarital birth, carried a strong message about the risks of premarital sex and created an intact family for the child.

Consequently, children did not have to worry much about losing a parent through divorce or never having had one because of nonmarital birth. After a surge in divorces following the Second World War, the rate leveled off. Only 11 percent of children born in the 1950s would by the time they turned eighteen see their parents separate or divorce. Out-of-wedlock childbirth barely figured as a cause of family disruption. In the 1950s and early 1960s, five percent of the nation's births were out of wedlock. Blacks were more likely than whites to bear children outside marriage, but the majority of black children born in the twenty years after the Second World War were born to married couples.

The rate of family disruption reached a historic low point during those years.

A new standard of family security and stability was established in postwar America. For the first time in history the vast majority of the nation's children could expect to live with married biological parents throughout childhood. Children might still suffer other forms of adversity—poverty, racial discrimination, lack of educational opportunity—but only a few would be deprived of the nurture and protection of a mother and a father. No longer did children have to be haunted by the classic fears vividly dramatized in folklore and fable—that their parents would die, that they would have to live with a stepparent and stepsiblings, or that they would be abandoned. These were the years when the nation confidently boarded up orphanages and closed foundling hospitals, certain that such institutions would never again be needed. In movie theaters across the country parents and children could watch the drama of parental separation and death in the great Disney classics, secure in the knowledge that such nightmare visions as the death of Bambi's mother and the wrenching separation of Dumbo from his mother were only make-believe.

In the 1960s the rate of family disruption suddenly began to rise. After inching up over the course of a century, the divorce rate soared. Throughout the 1950s and early 1960s the divorce rate held steady at fewer than ten divorces a year per 1,000 married couples. Then, beginning in about 1965, the rate increased sharply, peaking at twenty-three divorces per 1,000 marriages by 1979. (In 1974 divorce passed death as the leading cause of family breakup.) The rate has leveled off at about twenty-one divorces per 1,000 marriages—the figure for 1991. The out-of-wedlock birth rate also jumped. It went from five percent in 1960 to 27 percent in 1990. In 1990 close to 57 percent of births among black mothers were nonmarital, and about 17 percent among white mothers. Altogether, about one out of every four women who had a child in 1990 was not married. With rates of divorce and nonmarital birth so high, family disruption is at its peak. Never before have so many children experienced family breakup caused by events other than death. Each year a million children go through divorce or separation and almost as many more are born out of wedlock.

Half of all marriages now end in divorce. Following divorce, many people enter new relationships. Some begin living together. Nearly half of all cohabiting couples have children in the house-

hold. Fifteen percent have new children together. Many cohabiting couples eventually get married. However, both cohabiting and
remarried couples are more likely to break up than couples in
first marriages. Even social scientists find it hard to keep pace
with the complexity and velocity of such patterns. In the revised
edition (1992) of his book *Marriage, Divorce, Remarriage,* the sociologist Andrew Cherlin ruefully comments: "If there were a
truth-in-labeling law for books, the title of this edition should be
something long and unwieldly like *Cohabitation, Marriage, Divorce,
More Cohabitation, and Probably Remarriage.*"

Under such conditions growing up can be a turbulent experience. In many single-parent families children must come to terms
with the parent's love life and romantic partners. Some children
live with cohabiting couples, either their own unmarried parents
or a biological parent and a live-in partner. Some children born to
cohabiting parents see their parents break up. Others see their
parents marry, but 56 percent of them (as compared with 31
percent of the children born to married parents) later see their
parents' marriages fall apart. All told, about three quarters of
children born to cohabiting couples will live in a single-parent
home at least briefly. One of every four children growing up in
the 1990s will eventually enter a stepfamily. According to one
survey, nearly half of all children in stepparent families will see
their parents divorce again by the time they reach their late teens.
Since 80 percent of divorced fathers remarry, things get even
more complicated when the romantic or marital history of the
noncustodial parent, usually the father, is taken into account.
Consequently, as it affects a significant number of children, family disruption is best understood not as a single event but as a
string of disruptive events: separation, divorce, life in a single-
parent family, life with a parent and live-in lover, the remarriage
of one or both parents, life in one stepparent family combined
with visits to another stepparent family, the breakup of one or
both stepparent families. And so on. This is one reason why public schools have a hard time knowing whom to call in an emergency.

Given its dramatic impact on children's lives, one might reasonably expect that this historic level of family disruption would
be viewed with alarm, even regarded as a national crisis. Yet this
has not been the case. In recent years some people have argued
that these trends pose a serious threat to children and to the
nation as a whole, but they are dismissed as declinists, pessimists,

or nostalgists, unwilling or unable to accept the new facts of life. The dominant view is that the changes in family structure are, on balance, positive.

A Shift in the Social Metric

There are several reasons why this is so, but the fundamental reason is that at some point in the 1970s Americans changed their minds about the meaning of these disruptive behaviors. What had once been regarded as hostile to children's best interests was now considered essential to adults' happiness. In the 1950s most Americans believed that parents should stay in an unhappy marriage for the sake of the children. The assumption was that a divorce would damage the children, and the prospect of such damage gave divorce its meaning. By the mid-1970s a majority of Americans rejected that view. Popular advice literature reflected the shift. A book on divorce published in the mid-1940s tersely asserted: "Children are entitled to the affection and *association* of two parents, not one." Thirty years later another popular divorce book proclaimed just the opposite: "A two-parent home is not the only emotional structure within which a child can be happy and healthy. . . . The parents who take care of themselves will be best able to take care of their children." At about the same time, the long-standing taboo against out-of-wedlock childbirth also collapsed. By the mid-1970s three fourths of Americans said that it was not morally wrong for a woman to have a child outside marriage.

Once the social metric shifts from child well-being to adult well-being, it is hard to see divorce and nonmarital birth in anything but a positive light. However distressing and difficult they may be, both of these behaviors can hold out the promise of greater adult choice, freedom, and happiness. For unhappy spouses, divorce offers a way to escape a troubled or even abusive relationship and make a fresh start. For single parents, remarriage is a second try at marital happiness as well as a chance for relief from the stress, loneliness, and economic hardship of raising a child alone. For some unmarried women, nonmarital birth is a way to beat the biological clock, avoid marrying the wrong man, and experience the pleasures of motherhood. Moreover, divorce and out-of-wedlock birth involve a measure of agency and choice; they are man-and woman-made events. To be sure, not everyone exercises choice in divorce or nonmarital birth. Men leave wives for younger women, teenage girls get pregnant accidentally—yet even these unhappy events reflect the expansion of the boundaries of freedom and choice.

This cultural shift helps explain what otherwise would be inexplicable: the failure to see the rise in family disruption as a severe and troubling national problem. It explains why there is virtually no widespread public sentiment for restigmatizing either of these classically disruptive behaviors and no sense—no public consensus—that they can or should be avoided in the future. On the contrary, the prevailing opinion is that we should accept the changes in family structure as inevitable and devise new forms of public and private support for single-parent families.

The View From Hollywood

With its affirmation of the liberating effects of divorce and nonmarital childbirth, this opinion is a fixture of American popular culture today. Madison Avenue and Hollywood did not invent these behaviors, as their highly paid publicists are quick to point out, but they have played an influential role in defending and even celebrating divorce and unwed motherhood. More precisely, they have taken the raw material of demography and fashioned it into a powerful fantasy of individual renewal and rebirth. Consider, for example, the teaser for *People* magazine's cover story on Joan Lunden's divorce: "After the painful end of her 13-year marriage, the *Good Morning America* cohost is discovering a new life as a single mother—and as her own woman." *People* does not dwell on the anguish Lunden and her children might have experienced over the breakup of their family, or the difficulties of single motherhood, even for celebrity mothers. Instead, it celebrates Joan Lunden's steps toward independence and a better life. *People*, characteristically, focuses on her shopping: in the first weeks after her breakup Lunden leased "a brand-new six-bedroom, 8,000 square foot" house and then went to Bloomingdale's, where she scooped up sheets, pillows, a toaster, dishes, seven televisions, and roomfuls of fun furniture that was "totally unlike the serious traditional pieces she was giving up."

This is not just the view taken in supermarket magazines. Even the conservative bastion of the greeting-card industry, Hallmark, offers a line of cards commemorating divorce as liberation. "Think of your former marriage as a record album," says one

Contemporary card. "It was full of music—both happy and sad. But what's important now is . . . YOU! the recently released HOT, NEW, SINGLE! You're going to be at the TOP OF THE CHARTS!" Another card reads: "Getting divorced can be very healthy! Watch how it improves your circulation! Best of luck! . . . " Hallmark's hip Shoebox Greetings division depicts two female praying mantises. Mantis One: "It's tough being a single parent." Mantis Two: "Yeah . . . Maybe we shouldn't have eaten our husbands."

Divorce is a tired convention in Hollywood, but unwed parenthood is very much in fashion: in the past year or so babies were born to Warren Beatty and Annette Bening, Jack Nicholson and Rebecca Broussard, and Eddie Murphy and Nicole Mitchell. *Vanity Fair* celebrated Jack Nicolson's fatherhood with a cover story (April, 1992) called "Happy Jack." What made Jack happy, it turned out, was no-fault fatherhood. He and Broussard, the twenty-nine-year-old mother of his children, lived in separate houses. Nicholson said, "It's an unusual arrangement, but the last twenty-five years or so have shown me that I'm not good at cohabitation. . . . I see Rebecca as much as any other person who is cohabiting. And *she* prefers it. I think most people would in a more honest and truthful world." As for more-permanent commitments, the man who is not good at cohabitation said: "I don't discuss marriage much with Rebecca. Those discussions are the very thing I'm trying to avoid. I'm after this immediate real thing. That's all I believe in." (Perhaps Nicholson should have had the discussion. Not long after the story appeared, Broussard broke off the relationship.)

As this story shows, unwed parenthood is thought of not only as a way to find happiness but also as a way to exhibit such virtues as honesty and courage. A similar argument was offered in defense of Murphy Brown's unwed motherhood. Many of Murphy's fans were quick to point out that Murphy suffered over her decision to bear a child out of wedlock. Faced with an accidental pregnancy and a faithless lover, she agonized over her plight and, after much mental anguish, bravely decided to go ahead. In short, having a baby without a husband represented a higher level of maternal devotion and sacrifice than having a baby with a husband. Murphy was not just exercising her rights as a woman; she was exhibiting true moral heroism.

On the night Murphy Brown became an unwed mother, 34 million Americans tuned in, and CBS posted a 35 percent share of the audience. The show did not stir significant protest at the grass roots and lost none of its advertisers. The actress Candice Bergen subsequently appeared on the cover of nearly every women's and news magazine in the country and received an honorary degree at the University of Pennsylvania as well as an Emmy award. The show's creator, Diane English, popped up in Hanes stocking ads. Judged by conventional measures of approval, Murphy Brown's motherhood was a hit at the box office.

Increasingly, the media depicts the married two-parent family as a source of pathology. According to a spate of celebrity memoirs and interviews, the married-parent family harbors terrible secrets of abuse, violence, and incest. A bumper sticker I saw in Amherst, Massachusetts, read UNSPOKEN TRADITIONAL FAMILY VALUES: ABUSE, ALCOHOLISM, INCEST. The pop therapist John Bradshaw explains away this generation's problems with the dictum that 96 percent of families are dysfunctional, made that way by the addicted society we live in. David Lynch creates a new aesthetic of creepiness by juxtaposing scenes of traditional family life with images of seduction and perversion. A Boston-area museum puts on an exhibit called "Goodbye to Apple Pie," featuring several artists' visions of child abuse, including one mixed-media piece with knives poking through a little girl's skirt. The piece is titled *Father Knows Best*.

No one would claim that two-parent families are free from conflict, violence, or abuse. However, the attempt to discredit the two-parent family can be understood as part of what Daniel Patrick Moynihan has described as a larger effort to accommodate higher levels of social deviance. "The amount of deviant behavior in American society has increased beyond the levels the community can 'afford to recognize,'" Moynihan argues. One response has been to normalize what was once considered deviant behavior, such as out-of-wedlock birth. An accompanying response has been to detect deviance in what once stood as a social norm, such as the married-couple family. Together these responses reduce the acknowledged levels of deviance by eroding earlier distinctions between the normal and the deviant.

Several recent studies describe family life in its postwar heyday as the seedbed of alcoholism and abuse. According to Stephanie Coontz, the author of the book *The Way We Never Were: American Families and the Nostalgia Trap,* family life for married mothers in the 1950s consisted of "booze, bowling, bridge, and boredom." Coontz writes: "Few would have guessed that radiant

Marilyn Van Derbur, crowned Miss American in 1958, had been sexually violated by her wealthy, respectable father from the time she was five until she was eighteen, when she moved away to college." Even the budget-stretching casserole comes under attack as a sign of culinary dysfunction. According to one food writer, this homely staple of postwar family life brings back images of "the good mother of the 50's . . . locked in Ozzie and Harriet land, unable to move past the canvas of a Corning Ware dish, the palette of a can of Campbell's soup, the mushy dominion of which she was queen."

Nevertheless, the popular portrait of family life does not simply reflect the views of a cultural elite, as some have argued. There is strong support at the grass roots for much of this view of family change. Survey after survey shows that Americans are less inclined than they were a generation ago to value sexual fidelity, lifelong marriage, and parenthood as worthwhile personal goals. Motherhood no longer defines adult womanhood, as everyone knows; equally important is the fact that fatherhood has declined as a norm for men. In 1976 less than half as many fathers as in 1957 said that providing for children was a life goal. The proportion of working men who found marriage and children burdensome and restrictive more than doubled in the same period. Fewer than half of all adult Americans today regard the idea of sacrifice for others as a positive moral virtue.

Dinosaurs Divorce

It is true that many adults benefit from divorce or remarriage. According to one study, nearly 80 percent of divorced women and 50 percent of divorced men say they are better off out of the marriage. Half of divorced adults in the same study report greater happiness. A competent self-help book called *Divorce and New Beginnings* notes the advantages of single parenthood: single parents can "develop their own interests, fulfill their own needs, choose their own friends and engage in social activities of their choice. Money, even if limited, can be spent as they see fit." Apparently, some women appreciate the opportunity to have children out of wedlock. "The real world, however, does not always allow women who are dedicated to their careers to devote the time and energy it takes to find—or be found by—the perfect husband and father wanna-be," one woman said in a letter to *The Washington Post*. A mother and chiropractor from Avon, Connecticut, explained her unwed maternity to an interviewer this way: "It is selfish, but this was something I needed to do for me."

There is very little in contemporary popular culture to contradict this optimistic view. But in a few small places another perspective may be found. Several racks down from its divorce cards, Hallmark offers a line of cards for children—To Kids With Love. These cards come six to a pack. Each card in the pack has a slightly different message. According to the package, the "thinking of you" messages will let a special kid "know how much you care." Though Hallmark doesn't quite say so, it's clear these cards are aimed at divorced parents. "I'm sorry I'm not always there when you need me but I hope you know I'm always just a phone call away." Another card reads: "Even though your dad and I don't live together anymore, I know he's still a very special part of your life. And as much as I miss you when you're not with me, I'm still happy that you two can spend time together."

Hallmark's messages are grounded in a substantial body of well-funded market research. Therefore it is worth reflecting on the divergence in sentiment between the divorce cards for adults and the divorce cards for kids. For grown-ups, divorce heralds new beginnings (A HOT NEW SINGLE). For children, divorce brings separation and loss ("I'm sorry I'm not always there when you need me").

An even more telling glimpse into the meaning of family disruption can be found in the growing children's literature on family dissolution. Take, for example, the popular children's book *Dinosaurs Divorce: A Guide for Changing Families* (1986), by Laurence Krasny Brown and Marc Brown. This is a picture book, written for very young children. The book begins with a short glossary of "divorce words" and encourages children to "see if you can find them" in the story. The words include "family counselor," "separation agreements," "alimony," and "child custody." The book is illustrated with cartoonish drawings of green dinosaur parents who fight, drink too much, and break up. One panel shows the father dinosaur, suitcase in hand, getting into a yellow car.

The dinosaur children are offered simple, straightforward advice on what to do about the divorce. *On custody decisions:* "When parents can't agree, lawyers and judges decide. Try to be honest if they ask you questions; it will help them make better decisions." *On selling the house:* "If you move, you may have to say good-bye to friends and familiar places. But soon your new home will feel like the place you really belong." *On the economic impact of divorce:* "Living with one parent almost always means there will be less money. Be prepared to give up some things." *On holidays:* "Divorce may mean twice as much celebrating at holiday times, but you may feel pulled apart." *On parents' new lovers:* "You may sometimes feel jealous and want your parent to yourself. Be polite to your parents' new friends, even if you don't like them at first." *On parents' remarriage:* "Not everyone loves his or her stepparents, but showing them respect is important."

These cards and books point to an uncomfortable and generally unacknowledged fact: what contributes to a parent's happiness may detract from a child's happiness. All too often the adult quest for freedom, independence, and choice in family relationships conflicts with a child's developmental needs for stability, constancy, harmony, and permanence in family life. In short, family disruption creates a deep division between parents' interests and the interests of children.

One of the worst consequences of these divided interests is a withdrawal of parental investment in children's well-being. As the Stanford economist Victor Fuchs has pointed out, the main source of social investment in children is private. The investment comes from the children's parents. But parents in disrupted families have less time, attention, and money to devote to their children. The single most important source of disinvestment has been the widespread withdrawal of financial support and involvement by fathers. Maternal investment, too, has declined, as women try to raise families on their own and work outside the home. Moreover, both mothers and fathers commonly respond to family breakup by investing more heavily in themselves and in their own personal and romantic lives.

Sometimes the tables are completely turned. Children are called upon to invest in the emotional well-being of their parents. Indeed, this seems to be the larger message of many of the children's books on divorce and remarriage. *Dinosaurs Divorce* asks children to be sympathetic, understanding, respectful, and polite to confused, unhappy parents. The sacrifice comes from the children: "Be prepared to give up some things." In the world of divorcing dinosaurs, the children rather than the grown-ups are the exemplars of patience, restraint, and good sense.

Three Seventies Assumptions

As it first took shape in the 1970s, the optimistic view of family change rested on three bold new assumptions. At that time, because the emergence of the changes in family life was so recent, there was little hard evidence to confirm or dispute these assumptions. But this was an expansive moment in American life.

The first assumption was an economic one: that a woman could now afford to be a mother without also being a wife. There were ample grounds for believing this. Women's work-force participation had been gradually increasing in the postwar period, and by the beginning of the 1970s women were a strong presence in the workplace. What's more, even though there was still a substantial wage gap between men and women, women had made considerable progress in a relatively short time toward better-paying jobs and greater employment opportunities. More women than ever before could aspire to serious careers as business executives, doctors, lawyers, airline pilots, and politicians. This circumstance, combined with the increased availability of child care, meant that women could take on the responsibilities of a breadwinner, perhaps even a sole breadwinner. This was particularly true for middle-class women. According to a highly regarded 1977 study by the Carnegie Council on Children, "The greater availability of jobs for women means that more middle-class children today survive their parents' divorce without a catastrophic plunge into poverty."

Feminists, who had long argued that the path to greater equality for women lay in the world of work outside the home, endorsed this assumption. In fact, for many, economic independence was a stepping-stone toward freedom from both men and marriage. As women began to earn their own money, they were less dependent on men or marriage, and marriage diminished in importance. In Gloria Steinem's memorable words, "A woman without a man is like a fish without a bicycle."

This assumption also gained momentum as the meaning of work changed for women. Increasingly, work had an expressive as well as an economic dimension: being a working mother not only gave you an income but also made you more interesting and fulfilled than a stay-at-home mother. Consequently, the optimistic economic scenario was driven by a cultural imperative. Women would achieve financial independence because, culturally as well as economically, it was the right thing to do.

The second assumption was that family disruption would not cause lasting harm to children and could actually enrich their lives. *Creative Divorce: A New Opportunity for Personal Growth,* a popular book of the seventies, spoke confidently to this point: "Children can survive any family crisis without permanent damage—and grow as human beings in the process. . . . " Moreover, single-parent and stepparent families created a more extensive kinship network than the nuclear family. This network would envelop children in a web of warm and supportive relationships. "Belonging to a stepfamily means there are more people in your life," a children's book published in 1982 notes. "More sisters and brothers, including the step ones. More people you think of as grandparents and aunts and uncles. More cousins. More neighbors and friends. . . . Getting to know and like so many people (and having them like you) is one of the best parts of what being in a stepfamily . . . is all about."

The third assumption was that the new diversity in family structure would make America a better place. Just as the nation has been strengthened by the diversity of its ethnic and racial groups, so it would be strengthened by diverse family forms. The emergence of these brave new families was but the latest chapter in the saga of American pluralism.

Another version of the diversity argument stated that the real problem was not family disruption itself but the stigma still attached to these emergent family forms. This lingering stigma placed children at psychological risk, making them feel ashamed or different; as the ranks of single-parent and stepparent families grew, children would feel normal and good about themselves.

These assumptions continue to be appealing, because they accord with strongly held American beliefs in social progress. Americans see progress in the expansion of individual opportunities for choice, freedom, and self-expression. Moreover, Americans identify progress with growing tolerance of diversity. Over the past half century, the pollster Daniel Yankelovich writes, the United States has steadily grown more open-minded and accepting of groups that were previously perceived as alien, untrustworthy, or unsuitable for public leadership or social esteem. One such group is the burgeoning number of single-parent and stepparent families.

The Education of Sara McLanahan

In 1981 Sara McLanahan, now a sociologist at Princeton University's Woodrow Wilson School, read a three-part series by Ken Auletta in *The New Yorker*. Later published as a book titled *The Underclass*, the series presented a vivid portrait of the drug addicts, welfare mothers, and school dropouts who took part in an education-and-training program in New York City. Many were the children of single mothers, and it was Auletta's clear implication that single-mother families were contributing to the growth of an underclass. McLanahan was taken aback by this notion. "It struck me as strange that he would be viewing single mothers at that level of pathology."

"I'd gone to graduate school in the days when the politically correct argument was that single-parent families were just another alternative family form, and it was fine," McLanahan explains, as she recalls the state of social-scientific thinking in the 1970s. Several empirical studies that were then current supported an optimistic view of family change. (They used tiny samples, however, and did not track the well-being of children over time.)

One, *All Our Kin*, by Carol Stack, was required reading for thousands of university students. It said that single mothers had strengths that had gone undetected and unappreciated by earlier researchers. The single-mother family, it suggested, is an economically resourceful and socially embedded institution. In the late 1970s McLanahan wrote a similar study that looked at a small sample of white single mothers and how they coped. "So I was very much of that tradition."

By the early 1980s, however, nearly two decades had passed since the changes in family life had begun. During the intervening years a fuller body of empirical research had emerged: studies that used large samples, or followed families through time, or did both. Moreover, several of the studies offered a child's-eye view of family disruption. The National Survey on Children, conducted by the psychologist Nicholas Zill, had set out in 1976 to track a large sample of children aged seven to eleven. It also interviewed the children's parents and teachers. It surveyed its subjects again in 1981 and 1987. By the time of its third round of interviews the eleven-year-olds of 1976 were the twenty-two-year-olds of 1987. The California Children of Divorce Study, directed by Judith Wallerstein, a clinical psychologist, had also been going on for a decade. E. Mavis Hetherington, of the University of Virginia, was conducting a similar study of children from both intact and divorced families. For the first time it was possible to test the optimistic view against a large and longitudinal body of evidence.

It was to this body of evidence that Sara McLanahan turned. When she did, she found little to support the optimistic view of single motherhood. On the contrary. When she published her findings with Irwin Garfinkel in a 1986 book, *Single Mothers and Their Children,* her portrait of single motherhood proved to be as troubling in its own way as Auletta's.

One of the leading assumptions of the time was that single motherhood was economically viable. Even if single mothers did face economic trials, they wouldn't face them for long, it was argued, because they wouldn't remain single for long: single motherhood would be a brief phase of three to five years, followed by marriage. Single mothers would be economically resilient: if they experienced setbacks, they would recover quickly. It was also said that single mothers would be supported by informal networks of family, friends, neighbors, and other single mothers. As McLanahan shows in her study, the evidence demolishes all these claims.

For the vast majority of single mothers, the economic spectrum turns out to be narrow, running between precarious and desperate. Half the single mothers in the United States live below the poverty line. (Currently, one out of ten married couples with children is poor.) Many others live on the edge of poverty. Even single mothers who are far from poor are likely to experience persistent economic insecurity. Divorce almost always brings a decline in the standard of living for the mother and children.

Moreover, the poverty experienced by single mothers is no more brief than it is mild. A significant number of all single mothers never marry or remarry. Those who do, do so only after spending roughly six years, on average, as single parents. For black mothers the duration is much longer. Only 33 percent of African-American mothers had remarried within ten years of separation. Consequently, single motherhood is hardly a fleeting event for the mother, and it is likely to occupy a third of the child's childhood. Even the notion that single mothers are knit together in economically supportive networks is not borne out by the evidence. On the contrary, single parenthood forces many women to be on the move, in search of cheaper housing and better jobs. This need-driven restless mobility makes it more difficult for them to sustain supportive ties to family and friends, let alone other single mothers.

Single-mother families are vulnerable not just to poverty but to a particularly debilitating form of poverty: welfare dependency. The dependency takes two forms: First, single mothers, particularly unwed mothers, stay on welfare longer than other welfare recipients. Of those never-married mothers who receive welfare benefits, almost 40 percent remain on the rolls for ten years or longer. Second, welfare dependency tends to be passed on from one generation to the next. McLanahan says, "Evidence on inter-generational poverty indicates that, indeed, offspring from [single-mother] families are far more likely to be poor and to form mother-only families than are offspring who live with two parents most of their pre-adult life." Nor is the intergenerational impact of single motherhood limited to African-Americans, as many people seem to believe. Among white families, daughters of single parents are 53 percent more likely to marry as teenagers, 111 percent more likely to have children as teenagers, 164 percent more likely to have a premarital birth, and 92 percent more likely to dissolve their own marriages. All these intergenerational consequences of single motherhood increase the likelihood of chronic welfare dependency.

McLanahan cites three reasons why single-mother families are so vulnerable economically. For one thing, their earnings are low. Second, unless the mothers are widowed, they don't receive public subsidies large enough to lift them out of poverty. And finally, they do not get much support from family members—especially the fathers of their children. In 1982 single white mothers received an average of $1,246 in alimony and child support, black mothers an average of $322. Such payments accounted for about 10 percent of the income of single white mothers and for about 3.5 percent of the income of single black mothers. These amounts were dramatically smaller than the income of the father in a two-parent family and also smaller than the income from a second earner in a two-parent family. Roughly 60 percent of single white mothers and 80 percent of single black mothers received no support at all.

Until the mid-1980s, when stricter standards were put in place, child-support awards were only about half to two-thirds what the current guidelines require. Accordingly, there is often a big difference in the living standards of divorced fathers and of divorced mothers with children. After divorce the average annual income of mothers and children is $13,500 for whites and $9,000 for nonwhites, as compared with $25,000 for white nonresident fathers and $13,600 for nonwhite nonresident fathers. Moreover, since child-support awards account for a smaller portion of the income of a high-earning father, the drop in living standards can be especially sharp for mothers who were married to upper-level managers and professionals.

Unwed mothers are unlikely to be awarded any child support at all, partly because the paternity of their children may not have been established. According to one recent study, only 20 percent of unmarried mothers receive child support.

Even if single mothers escape poverty, economic uncertainty remains a condition of life. Divorce brings a reduction in income and standard of living for the vast majority of single mothers. One study, for example, found that income for mothers and children declines on average about 30 percent, while fathers experience a 10 to 15 percent increase in income in the year following a separation. Things get even more difficult when fathers fail to meet their child-support obligations. As a result, many divorced mothers experience a wearing uncertainty about the family budget: whether the check will come in or not; whether new sneakers can be bought this month or not; whether the electric bill will be paid on time or not. Uncertainty about money triggers other kinds of uncertainty. Mothers and children often have to move to cheaper housing after a divorce. One study shows that about 38 percent of divorced mothers and their children move during the first year after a divorce. Even several years later the rate of moves for single mothers is about a third higher than the rate for two-parent families. It is also common for a mother to change her job or increase her working hours or both following a divorce. Even the composition of the household is likely to change, with other adults, such as boyfriends or babysitters, moving in and out.

All this uncertainty can be devastating to children. Anyone who knows children knows that they are deeply conservative creatures. They like things to stay the same. So pronounced is this tendency that certain children have been known to request the same peanut-butter-and-jelly sandwich for lunch for years on end. Children are particularly set in their ways when it comes to family, friends, neighborhoods, and schools. Yet when a family breaks up, all these things may change. The novelist Pat Conroy has observed that "each divorce is the death of a small civilization." No one feels this more acutely than children.

Sara McLanahan's investigation and others like it have helped to establish a broad consensus on the economic impact of family disruption on children. Most social scientists now agree that single motherhood is an important and growing cause of poverty, and that children suffer as a result. (They continue to argue, however, about the relationship between family structure and such economic factors as income inequality, the loss of jobs in the inner city, and the growth of low-wage jobs.) By the mid-1980s, however, it was clear that the problem of family disruption was not confined to the urban underclass, nor was its sole impact economic. Divorce and out-of-wedlock childbirth were affecting middle- and upper-class children, and these more privileged children were suffering negative consequences as well. It appeared that the problems associated with family breakup were far deeper and far more widespread than anyone had previously imagined.

The Missing Father

Judith Wallerstein is one of the pioneers in research on the long-term psychological impact of family disruption on children. The California Children of Divorce Study, which she directs, remains the most enduring study of the long-term effects of divorce on children and their parents. Moreover, it represents the best-known effort to look at the impact of divorce on middle-class children. The California children entered the study without pathological family histories. Before divorce they lived in stable, protected homes. And although some of the children did experience economic insecurity as the result of divorce, they were generally free from the most severe forms of poverty associated with family breakup. Thus the study and the resulting book (which Wallerstein wrote with Sandra Blakeslee), *Second Chances: Men, Women, and Children a Decade After Divorce* (1989), provide new insight into the consequences of divorce which are not associated with extreme forms of economic or emotional deprivation.

When, in 1971, Wallerstein and her colleagues set out to conduct clinical interviews with 131 children from the San Francisco area, they thought they were embarking on a short-term study. Most experts believed that divorce was like a bad cold. There was a phase of acute discomfort, and then a short recovery phase. According to the conventional wisdom, kids would be back on their feet in no time at all. Yet when Wallerstein met these children for a second interview more than a year later, she was amazed to discover that there had been no miraculous recovery. In fact, the children seemed to be doing worse.

The news that children did not "get over" divorce was not particularly welcome at the time. Wallerstein recalls, "We got angry letters from therapists, parents, and lawyers saying we were undoubtedly wrong. They said children are really much better off being released from an unhappy marriage. Divorce, they said, is a liberating experience." One of the main results of the California study was to overturn this optimistic view. In Wallerstein's cautionary words, "Divorce is deceptive. Legally it is a single event, but psychologically it is a chain—sometimes a never-ending chain—of events, relocations, and radically shifting relationships strung through time, a process that forever changes the lives of the people involved."

Five years after divorce more than a third of the children experienced moderate or severe depression. At ten years a significant number of the now young men and women appeared to be troubled, drifting, and underachieving. At fifteen years many of the thirtyish adults were struggling to establish strong love relationships of their own. In short, far from recovering from their parents' divorce, a significant percentage of these grownups were still suffering from its effects. In fact, according to Wallerstein, the long-term effects of divorce emerge at a time when young adults are trying to make their own decisions about love, marriage, and family. Not all children in the study suffered negative consequences. But Wallerstein's research presents a sobering picture of divorce. "The child of divorce faces many additional psychological burdens in addition to the normative tasks of growing up," she says.

Divorce not only makes it more difficult for young adults to establish new relationships. It also weakens the oldest primary relationship: that between parent and child. According to Wallerstein, "Parent-child relationships are permanently altered by divorce in ways that our society has not anticipated." Not only do children experience a loss of parental attention at the onset of divorce, but they soon find that at every stage of their development their parents are not available in the same way they once were. "In a reasonably happy intact family," Wallerstein observes, "the child gravitates first to one parent and then to the other, using skills and attributes from each in climbing the developmental ladder." In a divorced family, children find it "harder to find the needed parent at needed times." This may help explain why very young children suffer the most as the result of family disruption. Their opportunities to engage in this kind of ongoing process are the most truncated and compromised.

The father-child bond is severely, often irreparably, damaged in disrupted families. In a situation without historical precedent, an astonishing and disheartening number of American fathers are failing to provide financial support to their children. Often, more than the father's support check is missing. Increasingly, children are bereft of any contact with their fathers. According to the National Survey of Children, in disrupted families only one child in six, on average, saw his or her father as often as once a week in the past year. Close to half did not see their father at all in the past year. As time goes on, contact becomes even more infrequent. Ten years after a marriage breaks up, more than two thirds of children report not having seen their father for a year. Not surprisingly, when asked to name the "adults you look up to and admire," only 20 percent of children in single-parent families named their father, as compared with 52 percent of children in two-parent families. A favorite complaint among Baby Boom Americans is that their fathers were emotionally remote guys who worked hard, came home at night to eat supper, and didn't have much to say to or do with the kids. But the current generation has a far worse father problem: many of their fathers are vanishing entirely.

Even for fathers who maintain regular contact, the pattern of father-child relationships changes. The sociologists Andrew Cherlin and Frank Furstenberg, who have studied broken families, write that the fathers behave more like other relatives than like parents. Rather than helping with homework or carrying out a project with their children, nonresidential fathers are likely to take the kids shopping, to the movies, or out to dinner. Instead of providing steady advice and guidance, divorced fathers become "treat" dads.

Apparently—and paradoxically—it is the visiting relationship itself, rather than the frequency of visits, that is the real source of the problem. According to Wallerstein, the few children in the California study who reported visiting with their fathers once or twice a week over a ten-year period still felt rejected. The need to schedule a special time to be with the child, the repeated leave-takings, and the lack of connection to the child's regular, daily schedule leaves many fathers adrift, frustrated, and confused. Wallerstein calls the visiting father a parent without portfolio.

The deterioration in father-child bonds is most severe among children who experience divorce at an early age, according to a recent study. Nearly three quarters of the respondents, now young men and women, report having poor relationships with their fathers. Close to half have received psychological help, nearly a third have dropped out of high school, and about a quarter report having experienced high levels of problem behavior or emotional distress by the time they became young adults.

Long-Term Effects

Since most children live with their mothers after divorce, one might expect that the mother-child bond would remain unaltered and might even be strengthened. Yet research shows that the mother-child bond is also weakened as the result of divorce. Only half of the children who were close to their mothers before a divorce remained equally close after the divorce. Boys, particularly, had difficulties with their mothers. Moreover, mother-child relationships deteriorated over time. Whereas teenagers in disrupted families were no more likely than teenagers in intact families to report poor relationships with their mothers, 30 percent of young adults from disrupted families have poor relationships with their mothers, as compared with 16 percent of young adults from intact families. Mother-daughter relationships often deteriorate as the daughter reaches young adulthood. The only group in society that derives any benefit from these weakened parent-child ties is the therapeutic community. Young adults from disrupted families are nearly twice as likely as those from intact families to receive psychological help.

Some social scientists have criticized Judith Wallerstein's research because her study is based on a small clinical sample and does not include a control group of children from intact families. However, other studies generally support and strengthen her findings. Nicholas Zill has found similar long-term effects on children of divorce, reporting that "effects of marital discord and family disruption are visible twelve to twenty-two years later in poor relationships with parents, high levels of problem behavior, and an increased likelihood of dropping out of high school and receiving psychological help." Moreover Zill's research also found signs of distress in young women who seemed relatively well adjusted in middle childhood and adolescence. Girls in single-parent families are also at much greater risk for precocious sexuality, teenage marriage, teenage pregnancy, nonmarital birth, and divorce than are girls in two-parent families.

Zill's research shows that family disruption strongly affects school achievement as well. Children in disrupted families are nearly twice as likely as those in intact families to drop out of high school; among children who do drop out, those from disrupted families are less likely eventually to earn a diploma or a GED. Boys are at greater risk for dropping out than girls, and are also more likely to exhibit aggressive, acting-out behaviors. Other research confirms these findings. According to a study by the National Association of Elementary School Principals, 33 percent of two-parent elementary school students are ranked as high achievers, as compared with 17 percent of single-parent students. The children in single-parent families are also more likely to be truant or late or to have disciplinary action taken against them. Even after controlling for race, income, and religion, scholars find significant differences in educational attainment between children who grow up in intact families and children who do not. In his 1992 study *America's Smallest School: The Family,* Paul Barton shows that the proportion of two-patent families varies widely from state to state and is related to variations in academic achievement. North Dakota, for example, scores highest on the math-proficiency test and second highest on the two-parent-family scale. The District of Columbia is second lowest on the math test and lowest in the nation on the two-parent-family scale.

Zill notes that "while coming from a disrupted family significantly increases a young adult's risks of experiencing social, emotional or academic difficulties, it does not foreordain such difficulties. The majority of young people from disrupted families have successfully completed high school, do *not* currently display high levels of emotional distress or problem behavior, and enjoy reasonable relationships with their mothers." Nevertheless, a majority of these young adults do show maladjustment in their relationships with their fathers.

These findings underscore the importance of both a mother and a father in fostering the emotional well-being of children. Obviously, not all children in two-parent families are free from emotional turmoil, but few are burdened with the troubles that accompany family breakup. Moreover, as the sociologist Amitai Etzioni explains in a new book, *The Spirit of Community,* two parents in an intact family make up what might be called a mutually supportive education coalition. When both parents are present, they can play different, even contradictory, roles. One parent may goad the child to achieve, while the other may encourage the child to take time out to daydream or toss a football around. One may emphasize taking intellectual risks, while the other may insist on following the teacher's guidelines. At the same time, the parents regularly exchange information about the child's school problems and achievements, and have a sense of the overall educational mission. However, Etzioni writes,

The sequence of divorce followed by a succession of boy or girlfriends, a second marriage, and frequently another divorce and another turnover of partners often means a repeatedly disrupted educational coalition. Each change in participants involves a change in the educational agenda for the child. Each new partner cannot be expected to pick up the previous one's educational post and program. . . . As a result, changes in parenting partners mean, at best, a deep disruption in a child's education, though of course several disruptions cut deeper into the effectiveness of the educational coalition than just one.

The Bad News About Stepparents

Perhaps the most striking and potentially disturbing, new research has to do with children in stepparent families. Until quite recently the optimistic assumption was that children saw their lives improve when they became part of a stepfamily. When Nicholas Zill and his colleagues began to study the effects of remarriage on children, their working hypothesis was that stepparent families would make up for the shortcomings of the single-parent family. Clearly, most children are better off economically when they are able to share in the income of two adults. When a second adult joins the household, there may be a reduction in the time and work pressures on the single parent.

The research overturns this optimistic assumption, however. In general the evidence suggests that remarriage neither reproduces nor restores the intact family structure, even when it brings more income and a second adult into the household. Quite the contrary. Indeed, children living with stepparents appear to be even more disadvantaged than children living in a stable single-parent family. Other difficulties seem to offset the advantages of extra income and an extra pair of hands. However much of our modern sympathies reject the fairy-tale portrait of stepparents, the latest research confirms that the old stories are anthropologically quite accurate. Stepfamilies disrupt established loyalties, create new uncertainties, provoke deep anxieties, and sometimes threaten a child's physical safety as well as emotional security.

Parents and children may dramatically different interests in and expectations for a new marriage. For a single parent, remarriage brings new commitments, the hope of enduring love and happiness, and relief from stress and loneliness. For a child, the same event often provokes confused feelings of sadness, anger, and rejection. Nearly half the children in Wallerstein's study said they felt left out in their stepfamilies. The National Commission on Children, a bipartisan group headed by Senator John D. Rockefeller, of West Virginia, reported that children from stepfamilies were more likely to say they often feel lonely or blue than children from either single-parent or intact families. Children in stepfamilies were the most likely to report that they wanted more time with their mothers. When mothers remarry, daughters tend to have a harder time adjusting than sons. Evidently, boys often respond positively to a male presence in the household, while girls who have established close ties to their mother in a single-parent family often see the stepfather as a rival and an intruder. According to one study, boys in remarried families are less likely to drop out of school than boys in single-parent families, while the opposite is true for girls.

A large percentage of children do not even consider stepparents to be part of their families, according to the National Survey on Children. The NSC asked children, "When you think of your family, who do you include?" Only 10 percent of the children failed to mention a biological parent, but a third left out a stepparent. Even children who rarely saw their noncustodial parents almost always named them as family members. The weak sense of attachment is mutual. When parents were asked the same question, only one percent failed to mention a biological child, while 15 percent left out a stepchild. In the same study stepparents with both natural children and stepchildren said that it was harder for them to love their stepchildren than their biological children and that their children would have been better off if they had grown up with two biological parents.

One of the most severe risks associated with stepparent-child ties is the risk of sexual abuse. As Judith Wallerstein explains, "The presence of a stepfather can raise the difficult issue of a thinner incest barrier." The incest taboo is strongly reinforced, Wallerstein says, by knowledge of paternity and by the experience of caring for a child since birth. A stepfather enters the family without either credential and plays a sexual role as the mother's husband. As a result, stepfathers can pose a sexual risk to the children, especially to daughters. According to a study by the Canadian researchers Martin Daly and Margo Wilson, preschool children in stepfamilies are forty times as likely as children in intact families to suffer physical or sexual abuse. (Most of the sexual abuse was committed by a third party, such as a neighbor, a stepfather's male friend, or another nonrelative.) Stepfathers dis-

criminate in their abuse: they are far more likely to assault non-
biological children than their own natural children.

Sexual abuse represents the most extreme threat to children's
well-being. Stepfamilies also seem less likely to make the kind of
ordinary investments in the children that other families do. Although it is true that the stepfamily household has a higher income than the single-parent household, it does not follow that the
additional income is reliably available to the children. To begin
with, children's claim on stepparents' resources is shaky. Stepparents are not legally required to support stepchildren, so their
financial support of these children is entirely voluntary. Moreover, since stepfamilies are far more likely to break up than intact
families, particularly in the first five years, there is always the
risk—far greater than the risk of unemployment in an intact
family—that the second income will vanish with another divorce.
The financial commitment to a child's education appears weaker
in stepparent families, perhaps because the stepparent believes
that the responsibility for educating the child rests with the biological parent.

Similarly, studies suggest that even though they may have the
time, the parents in stepfamilies do not invest as much of it in
their children as the parents in intact families or even single parents do. A 1991 survey by the National Commission on Children
showed that the parents in stepfamilies were less likely to be involved in a child's school life, including involvement in extracur-
ricular activities, than either intact-family parents or single parents. They were the least likely to report being involved in such
time-consuming activities as coaching a child's team, accompanying class trips, or helping with school projects. According to
McLanahan's research, children in stepparent families report
lower educational aspirations on the part of their parents and
lower levels of parental involvement with schoolwork. In short, it
appears that family income and the number of adults in the
household are not the only factors affecting children's well-being.

Diminishing Investments

There are several reasons for this diminished interest and
investment. In the law, as in the children's eyes, stepparents are
shadowy figures. According to the legal scholar David Chambers,
family law has pretty much ignored stepparents. Chambers
writes, "In the substantial majority of states, stepparents, even

when they live with a child, have no legal obligation to contribute to the child's support; nor does a stepparent's presence in the home alter the support obligations of a noncustodial parent. The stepparent also has . . . no authority to approve emergency medical treatment or even to sign a permission slip. . . . " When a marriage breaks up, the stepparent has no continuing obligation to provide for a stepchild, no matter how long or how much he or she has been contributing to the support of the child. In short, Chambers says, stepparent relationships are based wholly on consent, subject to the inclinations of the adult and the child. The only way a stepparent can acquire the legal status of a parent is through adoption. Some researchers also point to the cultural ambiguity of the stepparent's role as a source of diminished interest, while others insist that it is the absence of a blood tie that weakens the bond between stepparent and child.

Whatever its causes, the diminished investment in children in both single-parent and stepparent families has a significant impact on their life chances. Take parental help with college costs. The parents in intact families are far more likely to contribute to children's college costs than are those in disrupted families. Moreover, they are usually able to arrive at a shared understanding of which children will go to college, where they will go, how much the parents will contribute, and how much the children will contribute. But when families break up, these informal understandings can vanish. The issue of college tuition remains one of the most contested areas of parental support, especially for higher-income parents.

The law does not step in even when familial understandings break down. In the 1980s many states lowered the age covered by child-support agreements from twenty-one to eighteen, thus eliminating college as a cost associated with support for a minor child. Consequently, the question of college tuition is typically not addressed in child-custody agreements. Even in states where the courts do require parents to contribute to college costs, the requirement may be in jeopardy. In a recent decision in Pennsylvania the court overturned an earlier decision ordering divorced parents to contribute to college tuition. This decision is likely to inspire challenges in other states where courts have required parents to pay for college. Increasingly, help in paying for college is entirely voluntary.

Judith Wallerstein has been analyzing the educational decisions of the college-age men and women in her study. She reports that "a full 42 percent of these men and women from middle class families appeared to have ended their educations without attempting college or had left college before achieving a degree at either the two-year or the four-year level." A significant percentage of these young people have the ability to attend college. Typical of this group are Nick and Terry, sons of a college professor. They had been close to their father before the divorce, but their father remarried soon after the divorce and saw his sons only occasionally, even though he lived nearby. At age nineteen Nick had completed a few junior-college courses and was earning a living as a salesman. Terry, twenty-one, who had been tested as a gifted student, was doing blue-collar work irregularly.

Sixty-seven percent of the college-age students from disrupted families attended college, as compared with 85 percent of other students who attended the same high schools. Of those attending college, several had fathers who were financially capable of contributing to college costs but did not.

The withdrawal of support for college suggests that other customary forms of parental help-giving, too, may decline as the result of family breakup. For example, nearly a quarter of first-home purchases since 1980 have involved help from relatives, usually parents. The median amount of help is $5,000. It is hard to imagine that parents who refuse to contribute to college costs will offer help in buying first homes, or help in buying cars or health insurance for young adult family members. And although it is too soon to tell, family disruption may affect the generational transmission of wealth. Baby Boomers will inherit their parents' estates, some substantial, accumulated over a lifetime by parents who lived and saved together. To be sure, the postwar generation benefited from an expanding economy and a rising standard of living, but its ability to accumulate wealth also owed something to family stability. The lifetime assets, like the marriage itself, remained intact. It is unlikely that the children of disrupted families will be in so favorable a position.

Moreover, children from disrupted families may be less likely to help their aging parents. The sociologist Alice Rossi, who has studied intergenerational patterns of help-giving, says that adult obligation has its roots in early-childhood experience. Children who grow up in intact families experience higher levels of obligation to kin than children from broken families. Children's sense of obligation to a nonresidential father is particularly weak. Among adults with both parents living, those separated from their father during childhood are less likely than others to see the father regularly. Half of them see their father more than once a year, as compared with nine out of ten of those whose parents are still married. Apparently a kind of bitter justice is at work here. Fathers who do not support or see their young children may not be able to count on their adult children's support when they are old and need money, love, and attention.

In short, as Andrew Cherlin and Frank Furstenburg put it, "Through divorce and remarriage, individuals are related to more and more people, to each of whom they owe less and less." Moreover, as Nicholas Zill argues, weaker parent-child attachments leave many children more strongly exposed to influences outside the family, such as peers, boyfriends or girlfriends, and the media. Although these outside forces can sometimes be helpful, common sense and research opinion argue against putting too much faith in peer groups or the media as surrogates for Mom and Dad.

Poverty, Crime, Education

Family disruption would be a serious problem even if it affected only individual children and families. But its impact is far broader. Indeed, it is not an exaggeration to characterize it as a central cause of many of our most vexing social problems. Consider three problems that most Americans believe rank among the nation's pressing concerns: poverty, crime, and declining school performance.

More than half of the increase in child poverty in the 1980s is attributable to changes in family structure, according to David Eggebeen and Daniel Lichter, of Pennsylvania State University. In fact, if family structure in the United States had remained relatively constant since 1960, the rate of child poverty would be a third lower than it is today. This does not bode well for the future. With more than half of today's children likely to live in single-parent families, poverty and associated welfare costs threaten to become even heavier burdens on the nation.

Crime in American cities has increased dramatically and grown more violent over recent decades. Much of this can be attributed to the rise in disrupted families. Nationally, more than 70 percent of all juveniles in state reform institutions come from fatherless homes. A number of scholarly studies find that even after the groups of subjects are controlled for income, boys from single-mother homes are significantly more likely than others to commit crimes and to wind up in the juvenile justice, court, and penitentiary systems. One such study summarizes the relationship between crime and one-parent families in this way: "The relationship is so strong that controlling for family configuration erases the relationship between race and crime and between low income and crime. This conclusion shows up time and again in the literature." The nation's mayors, as well as police officers, social workers, probation officers, and court officials, consistently pint to family breakup as the most important source of rising rates of crime.

Terrible as poverty and crime are, they tend to be concentrated in inner cities and isolated from the everyday experience of many Americans. The same cannot be said of the problem of declining school performance. Nowhere has the impact of family breakup been more profound or widespread than in the nation's public schools. There is a strong consensus that the schools are failing in their historic mission to prepare every American child to be a good worker and a good citizen. And nearly everyone agrees that the schools must undergo dramatic reform in order to reach that goal. In pursuit of that goal, moreover, we have suffered no shortage of bright ideas or pilot projects or bold experiments in school reform. But there is little evidence that measures such as curricular reform, school-based management, and school choice will address, let alone solve, the biggest problem schools face: the rising number of children who come from disrupted families.

The great educational tragedy of our time is that many American children are failing in school not because they are intellectually or physically impaired but because they are emotionally incapacitated. In schools across the nation principals report a dramatic rise in the aggressive, acting-out behavior characteristic of children, especially boys, who are living in single-parent families. The discipline problems in today's suburban schools—assaults on teachers, unprovoked attacks on other students, screaming outbursts in class—outstrip the problems that were evident in the toughest city schools a generation ago. Moreover, teachers find many children emotionally distracted, so upset and preoccupied by the explosive drama of their own family lives that they are unable to concentrate on such mundane matters as multiplication tables.

In response, many schools have turned to therapeutic remediation. A growing proportion of many school budgets is devoted to counseling and other psychological services. The curriculum is becoming more therapeutic: children are taking courses in self-esteem, conflict resolution, and aggression management. Parental advisory groups are conscientiously debating alternative approaches to traditional school discipline, ranging from teacher training in mediation to the introduction of metal detectors and security guards in the schools. Schools are increasingly becoming emergency rooms of the emotions, devoted not only to developing minds but also to repairing hearts. As a result, the mission of the school, along with the culture of the classroom, is slowly changing. What we are seeing, largely as a result of the new burdens of family disruption, is the psychologization of American education.

Taken together, the research presents a powerful challenge to the prevailing view of family change as social progress. Not a single one of the assumptions underlying that view can be sustained against the empirical evidence. Single-parent families are not able to do well economically on a mother's income. In fact, most teeter on the economic brink, and many fall into poverty and welfare dependency. Growing up in a disrupted family does not enrich a child's life or expand the number of adults committed to the child's well-being. In fact, disrupted families threaten the psychological well-being of children and diminish the investment of adult time and money in them. Family diversity in the form of increasing numbers of single-parent and stepparent families does not strengthen the social fabric. It dramatically weakens and undermines society, placing new burdens on schools, courts, prisons, and the welfare system. These new families are not an improvement on the nuclear family, nor are they even just as good, whether you look at outcomes for children or outcomes for society as a whole. In short, far from representing social progress, family change represents a stunning example of social regress.

The Two-Parent Advantage

All this evidence gives rise to an obvious conclusion: growing up in an intact two-parent family is an important source of advantage for American children. Though far from perfect as a social institution, the intact family offers children greater security and better outcomes than its fast-growing alternatives: single-parent and stepparent families. Not only does the intact family protect the child from poverty and economic insecurity; it also provides greater noneconomic investments of parental time, attention, and emotional support over the entire life course. This does not mean that all two-parent families are better for children than all single-parent families. But in the face of the evidence it becomes increasingly difficult to sustain the proposition that all family structures produce equally good outcomes for children.

Curiously, many in the research community are hesitant to say that two-parent families generally promote better outcomes for children than single-parent families. Some argue that we need finer measures of the extent of the family-structure effect. As one scholar has noted, it is possible, by disaggregating the data in certain ways, to make family structure "go away" as an independent variable. Other researchers point to studies that show that children suffer psychological effects as a result of family conflict preceding family breakup. Consequently, they reason, it is the conflict rather than the structure of the family that is responsible for many of the problems associated with family disruption. Others, including Judith Wallerstein, caution against treating children in divorced families and children in intact families as separate populations, because doing so tends to exaggerate the differences between the two groups. "We have to take this family by family," Wallerstein says.

Some of the caution among researchers can also be attributed to ideological pressures. Privately, social scientists worry that their research may serve ideological causes that they themselves do not support, or that their work may be misinterpreted as an attempt to "tell people what to do." Some are fearful that they will be attacked by feminist colleagues, or, more generally, that their comments will be regarded as an effort to turn back the clock to the 1950s—a goal that has almost no constituency in the academy. Even more fundamental, it has become risky for anyone—scholar, politician, religious leader—to make normative statements today. This reflects not only the persistent drive toward "value neutrality" in the professions but also a deep confusion about the purposes of public discourse. The dominant view appears to be that social criticism, like criticism of individuals, is psychologically damaging. The worst thing you can do is to make people feel guilty or bad about themselves.

When one sets aside these constraints, however, the case against the two-parent family is remarkably weak. It is true that disaggregating data can make family structure less significant as a factor, just as disaggregating Hurricane Andrew into wind, rain, and tides can make it disappear as a meterological phenomenon. Nonetheless, research opinion as well as common sense suggests that the effects of changes in family structure are great enough to cause concern. Nicholas Zill argues that many of the risk factors for children are doubled or more than doubled as the result of family disruption. "In epidemiological terms," he writes, "the doubling of a hazard is a substantial increase. . . . the increase in risk that dietary cholesterol poses for cardiovascular disease, for example, is far less than double, yet millions of Americans have altered their diets because of the perceived hazard."

The argument that family conflict, rather than the breakup of parents, is the cause of children's psychological distress is persuasive on its face. Children who grow up in high-conflict families, whether the families stay together or eventually split up, are undoubtedly at great psychological risk. And surely no one would dispute that there must be societal measures available, including divorce, to remove children from families where they are in danger. Yet only a minority of divorces grow out of pathological situations; much more common are divorces in families unscarred by physical assault. Moreover, an equally compelling hypothesis is that family breakup generates its own conflict. Certainly, many families exhibit more conflictual and even violent behavior as a consequence of divorce than they did before divorce.

Finally, it is important to note that clinical insights are different from sociological findings. Clinicians work with individual families, who cannot and should not be defined by statistical aggregates. Appropriate to a clinical approach, moreover, is a focus on the internal dynamics of family functioning and on the immense variability in human behavior. Nevertheless, there is enough empirical evidence to justify sociological statements about the causes of declining child well-being and to demonstrate that despite the plasticity of human response, there are some useful rules of thumb to guide our thinking about and policies affecting the family.

For example, Sara McLanahan says, three structural constants are commonly associated with intact families, even intact families who would not win any "Family of the Year" awards. The first is economic. In intact families, children share in the income of two adults. Indeed, as a number of analysts have pointed out, the two-parent family is becoming more rather than less necessary, because more and more families need two incomes to sustain a middle-class standard of living.

McLanahan believes that most intact families also provide a stable authority structure. Family breakup commonly upsets the established boundaries of authority in a family. Children are often required to make decisions or accept responsibilities once considered the province of parents. Moreover, children, even very young children, are often expected to behave like mature adults, so that the grown-ups in the family can be free to deal with the emotional fallout of the failed relationship. In some instances family disruption creates a complete vacuum in authority; everyone invents his or her own rules. With lines of authority disrupted or absent, children find it much more difficult to engage in the normal kinds of testing behavior, the trial and error, the failing and succeeding, that define the developmental pathway toward character and competence. McLanahan says, "Children need to be the ones to challenge the rules. The parents need to set the boundaries and let the kids push the boundaries. The children shouldn't have to walk the straight and narrow at all times."

Finally, McLanahan holds that children in intact families benefit from stability in what she neutrally terms "household personnel." Family disruption frequently brings new adults into the family, including stepparents, live-in boyfriends or girlfriends, and casual sexual partners. Like stepfathers, boyfriends can present a real threat to children's, particularly to daughters', security and well-being. But physical or sexual abuse represents only the most extreme such threat. Even the very best of boyfriends can disrupt and undermine a child's sense of peace and security, McLanahan says. "It's not as though you're going from an unhappy marriage to peacefulness. There can be a constant changing until the mother finds a suitable partner."

McLanahan's argument helps explain why children of widows tend to do better than children of divorced or unmarried mothers. Widows differ from other single mothers in all three respects. They are economically more secure, because they receive more public assistance through Survivors Insurance, and possibly private insurance or other kinds of support from family members. Thus widows are less likely to leave the neighborhood in search of a new or better job and a cheaper house or apartment. Moreover, the death of a father is not likely to disrupt the authority structure radically. When a father dies, he is no longer physically present, but his death does not dethrone him as an authority figure in the child's life. On the contrary, his authority may be magnified through death. The mother can draw on the powerful memory of the departed father as a way of intensifying her parental authority: "Your father would have wanted it this way." Finally, since widows tend to be older than divorced mothers, their love life may be less distracting.

Regarding the two-parent family, the sociologist David Popenoe, who has devoted much of his career to the study of families, both in the United States and in Scandinavia, makes this straightforward assertion:

Social science research is almost never conclusive. There are always methodological difficulties and stones left unturned. Yet in three decades of work as a social scientist, I know of few other bodies of data in which the weight of evidence is so decisively on one side of the issue: on the whole, for children, two-parent families are preferable to single-parent and stepfamilies.

The Regime Effect

The rise in family disruption is not unique to American society. It is evident in virtually all advanced nations, including Japan, where it is also shaped by the growing participation of women in the work force. Yet the United States has made divorce easier and quicker than in any other Western nation with the sole exception of Sweden—and the trend toward solo motherhood has also been more pronounced in America. (Sweden has an equally high rate of out-of-wedlock birth, but the majority of such births are to cohabiting couples, a long-established pattern in Swedish society.) More to the point, nowhere has family breakup been greeted by a more triumphant rhetoric of renewal than in America.

What is striking about this rhetoric is how deeply it reflects classic themes in American public life. It draws its language and imagery from the nation's founding myth. It depicts family breakup as a drama of revolution and rebirth. The nuclear family represents the corrupt past, an institution guilty of the abuse of power and the suppression of individual freedom. Breaking up the family is like breaking away from Old World tyranny. Liberated from the bonds of the family, the individual can achieve independence and experience a new beginning, a fresh start, a new birth of freedom. In short, family breakup recapitulates the American experience.

This rhetoric is an example of what the University of Maryland political philosopher William Galston has called the "regime

effect." The founding of the United States set in motion a new
political order based to an unprecedented degree on individual
rights, personal choice, and egalitarian relationships. Since then
these values have spread beyond their original domain of political
relationships to define social relationships as well. During the past
twenty-five years these values have had a particularly profound
impact on the family.

Increasingly, political principles of individual rights and
choice shape our understanding of family commitment and solidarity. Family relationships are viewed not as permanent or bind-
ing but as voluntary and easily terminable. Moreover, under the
sway of the regime effect the family loses its central importance as
an institution in the civil society, accomplishing certain social goals
such as raising children and caring for its members, and becomes
a means to achieving greater individual happiness—a lifestyle
choice. Thus, Galston says, what is happening to the American
family reflects the "unfolding logic of authoritative, deeply
American moral-political principles."

One benefit of the regime effect is to create greater equality
in adult family relationships. Husbands and wives, mothers and
fathers, enjoy relationships far more egalitarian than past relationships were, and most Americans prefer it that way. But the
political principles of the regime effect can threaten another kind
of family relationship—that between parent and child. Owing
to their biological and developmental immaturity, children are
needy dependents. They are not able to express their choices
according to limited, easily terminable, voluntary agreements.
They are not able to act as negotiators in family decisions, even
those that most affect their own interests. As one writer has put it,
"a newborn does not make a good 'partner.'" Correspondingly,
the parental role is antithetical to the spirit of the regime. Parental investment in children involves a diminished investment in
self, a willing deference to the needs and claims of the dependent
child. Perhaps more than any other family relationship, the
parent-child relationship—shaped as it is by patterns of dependency and deference—can be undermined and weakened by the
principles of the regime.

More than a century and a half ago Alexis de Tocqueville
made the striking observation that an individualistic society depends on a communitarian institution like the family for its continued existence. The family cannot be constituted like the liberal
state, nor can it be governed entirely by that state's principles. Yet

the family serves as the seedbed for the virtues required by a liberal state. The family is responsible for teaching lessons of independence, self-restraint, responsibility, and right conduct, which are essential to a free, democratic society. If the family fails in these tasks, then the entire experiment in democratic self-rule is jeopardized.

To take one example: independence is basic to successful functioning in American life. We assume that most people in America will be able to work, care for themselves and their families, think for themselves, and inculcate the same traits of independence and initiative in their children. We depend on families to teach people to do these things. The erosion of the two-parent family undermines the capacity of families to impart this knowledge; children of long-term welfare-dependent single parents are far more likely than others to be dependent themselves. Similarly, the children in disrupted families have a harder time forging bonds of trust with others and giving and getting help across the generations. This, too, may lead to greater dependency on the resources of the state.

Over the past two and a half decades Americans have been conducting what is tantamount to a vast natural experiment in family life. Many would argue that this experiment was necessary, worthwhile, and long overdue. The results of the experiment are coming in, and they are clear. Adults have benefited from the changes in family life in important ways, but the same cannot be said for children. Indeed, this is the first generation in the nation's history to do worse psychologically, socially, and economically than its parents. Most poignantly, in survey after survey the children of broken families confess deep longings for an intact family.

Nonetheless, as Galston is quick to point out, the regime effect is not an irresistible undertow that will carry away the family. It is more like a swift current, against which it is possible to swim. People learn; societies can change, particularly when it becomes apparent that certain behaviors damage the social ecology, threaten the public order, and impose new burdens on core institutions. Whether Americans will act to overcome the legacy of family disruption is a crucial but as yet unanswered question.

BRINGING UP FATHER[3]

"I don't have a dad," says Megan, 8, a tiny blond child with a pixie nose who gazes up at a visitor and talks of her hunger. "Well, I do have a dad, but I don't know his name. I only know his first name, Bill."

Just what is it that fathers do?

"Love you. They kiss you and hug you when you need them. I had my mom's boyfriend for a while, but they broke up." Now Megan lives with just her mother and older brother in Culver City, California.

What would you like to do with your dad?

"I'd want him to talk to me." She's hurting now. "I wish I had somebody to talk to. It's not fair. If two people made you, then you should still be with those two people." And she's sad. "I'm not so special," she says, looking down at the floor. "I don't have two people."

She imagines what it would be like for him to come home from work at night.

"It would be just like that commercial where the kids say, 'Daddy, are you all right?'" She smiles, dreaming. "The kids show the daddy that they care for him. They put a thermometer in his mouth. They think he's sick because he came home early. They are sitting on the couch watching TV, and it's like, wow, we can play with Dad!"

Megan thinks her father is in the Navy now. "One day when I get older, I'm gonna go back to Alabama and try to find him."

More children will go to sleep tonight in a fatherless home than ever in the nation's history. Talk to the experts in crime, drug abuse, depression, school failure, and they can point to some study somewhere blaming those problems on the disappearance of fathers from the American family. But talk to the fathers who do stay with their families, and the story grows more complicated. What they are hearing, from their bosses, from institutions, from the culture around them, even from their own wives, very often comes down to a devastating message: We don't really trust men to be parents, and we don't really need them to

[3]Article by Nancy R. Gibbs. From *Time* 141(26):52–61 Je 28 '93. Copyright © 1993 by Time, Inc. Reprinted with permission.

be. And so every day, everywhere, their children are growing up without them.

Corporate America, for a start, may praise family life but does virtually nothing to ease it. Managers still take male workers aside and warn them not to take a paternity leave if they want to be taken seriously. On TV and in movies and magazine ads, the image of fathers over the past generation evolved from the stern, sturdy father who knew best to a helpless Homer Simpson, or some ham-handed galoot confounded by the prospect of changing a diaper. Teachers call parent conferences but only talk to the mothers. When father arrives at the doctor's office with little Betsy, the pediatrician offers instructions to pass along to his wife, the caregiver presumptive. The Census Bureau can document the 70 million mothers age 15 or older in the U.S. but has scant idea how many fathers there are. "There's no interest in fathers at all," says sociologist Vaughn Call, who directs the National Survey of Families and Households at the University of Wisconsin. "It's a nonexistent category. It's the ignored half of the family."

Mothers themselves can be unwitting accomplices. Even women whose own progress in public life depends on sharing the workload in private life act as "gatekeepers" in the home, to use Harvard pediatrician T. Berry Brazelton's description. Dig deeply into household dynamics, and the tensions emerge. Women say they need and want their husbands to be more active parents but fear that they aren't always reliable. Men say they might like to be more involved, but their wives will not make room for them, and jealously guard their domestic power.

Most troubling of all to some social scientists is the message men get that being a good father means learning how to mother. Among child-rearing experts, the debate rages over whether men and women parent differently, whether there is some unique contribution that each makes to the emotional health of their children. "Society sends men two messages," says psychologist Jerrold Lee Shapiro, father of two and the author of *A Measure of the Man*, his third book on fatherhood. "The first is, We want you to be involved, but you'll be an inadequate mother. The second is, You're invited into the birthing room and into the nurturing process—but we don't want all of you. We only want your support. We're not really ready as a culture to accept men's fears, their anger or their sadness. This is the stuff that makes men crazy. We want men to be the protectors and providers, but we are scared they won't be if they become soft."

So now America finds its stereotypes crushed in the collision between private needs and public pressures. While some commend the nurturing nature of the idealized New Father, others cringe at the idea of genderless parenting and defend the importance of men being more than pale imitations of mothers. "If you become Mr. Mom," says Shapiro, "the family has a mother and an assistant mother. That isn't what good fathers are doing today." And fathers themselves wrestle with memories of their own fathers, vowing to do it differently, and struggling to figure out how.

The Disappearing Dad

Well into the 18th century, child-rearing manuals in America were generally addressed to fathers, not mothers. But as industrialization began to separate home and work, fathers could not be in both places at once. Family life of the 19th century was defined by what historians call the feminization of the domestic sphere and the marginalization of the father as a parent. By the 1830s, child-rearing manuals, increasingly addressed to mothers, deplored the father's absence from the home. In 1900 one worried observer could describe "the suburban husband father" as "almost entirely a Sunday institution."

What alarms modern social scientists is that in the latter part of this century the father has been sidelined in a new, more disturbing way. Today he's often just plain absent. Rising divorce rates and out-of-wedlock births mean that more than 40% of all children born between 1970 and 1984 are likely to spend much of their childhood living in single-parent homes. In 1990, 25% were living with only their mothers, compared with 5% in 1960. Says David Blankenhorn, the founder of the Institute of American Values in New York City: "This trend of fatherlessness is the most socially consequential family trend of our generation."

Credit Dan Quayle for enduring the ridicule that opened the mainstream debate over whether fathers matter in families. In the year since his famous Murphy Brown speech, social scientists have produced mounting evidence that, at the very least, he had a point. Apart from the personal politics of parenting, there are larger social costs to reckon in a society that dismisses fathers as luxuries.

Studies of young criminals have found that more than 70% of all juveniles in state reform institutions come from fatherless homes. Children from broken families are nearly twice as likely as those in two-parent families to drop out of high school. After assessing the studies, economist Sylvia Hewlett suggested that "school failure may well have as much to do with disintegration of families as with the quality of schools."

Then there is the emotional price that children pay. In her 15 years tracking the lives of children of divorced families, Judith Wallerstein found that five years after the split, more than a third experienced moderate or severe depression. After 10 years a significant number of the young men and women appeared to be troubled, drifting and underachieving. At 15 years many of the thirtyish adults were struggling to create strong love relationships of their own. Daughters of divorce, she found, "often experience great difficulty establishing a realistic view of men in general, developing realistic expectations, and exercising good judgment in their choice of partners."

For boys, the crucial issue is role modeling. There are psychologists who suggest that boys without fathers risk growing up with low self-esteem, becoming overly dependent on women and emotionally rigid. "Kids without fathers are forced to find their own ways of doing things," observes Melissa Manning, a social worker at the Boys and Girls Club of Venice, California. "So they come up with their own ideas, from friends and from the gangs. Nobody is showing them what to do except to be drunk, deal drugs or go to jail." Then there are the subtler lessons that dads impart. Attorney Charles Firestone, for instance, recently decided it was time to teach his 11-year-old son how to play poker. "Maybe it will help if he knows when to hold 'em, when to fold 'em," he says.

The Anti-Father Message

Given the evidence that men are so vital to a healthy home, the anti-father messages that creep into the culture and its institutions are all the more troubling. Some scholars suggest that fatherhood is by its very biological nature more fragile than motherhood, and needs to be encouraged by the society around it. And yet for all the focus on the New Father (the kind who skips the corporate awards dinner to attend the school play), the messages men receive about how they should act as parents are at best mixed and often explicitly hostile.

Employers that have been slow to accommodate the needs of mothers in their midst are often even more unforgiving of fathers. It is a powerful taboo that prevents men from acknowledging their commitment to their children at work. A 1989 survey of medium and large private employers found that only 1% of employees had access to paid paternity leave and just 18% could take unpaid leave. Even in companies like Eastman Kodak, only 7% of men, vs. 93% of women, have taken advantage of the six-year-old family-leave plan.

Those who do soon discover the cost. "My boss made me pay a price for it emotionally," says a prominent Washington executive who took leaves for both his children. "He was very generous with the time, but he never let me forget it. Every six seconds he reminded me what a great guy he was and that I owed him really, really big. You don't get a lot of points at the office for wanting to have a healthy family life." Men, like women, are increasingly troubled by the struggle to balance home and work; in 1989, asked if they experienced stress while doing so, 72% of men answered yes, compared with 12% a decade earlier, according to James Levine of the Fatherhood Project at the Families and Work Institute of New York City.

Many men will freely admit that they sometimes lie to employers about their commitments. "I announced that I was going to a meeting," shrugged a Washington journalist as he left the office in midafternoon one day recently. "I just neglected to mention that the 'meeting' was to watch my daughter play tennis." Now it is the fathers who are beginning to ask themselves whether their careers will stall and their incomes stagnate, whether the glass ceiling will press down on them once they make public their commitment as parents, whether today's productivity pressures will force them to work even harder with that much less time to be with their kids. In the higher reaches of management, there are not only few women, there are also few men in dual-income families who take an active part in raising their children. "Those who get to the top today," says Charles Rodgers, owner of a 10-year-old family-research organization in Brookline, Massachusetts, called Work/Family Directions, "are almost always men from what used to be the traditional family, men with wives who don't work outside the home."

Many men insist that they long to veer off onto a "daddy track." In a 1990 poll by the Los Angeles *Times*, 39% of the fathers said they would quit their jobs to have more time with their kids, while another survey found that 74% of men said they would rather have a daddy-track job than a fast-track job. But in real life, when they are not talking to pollsters, some fathers recognize the power of their atavistic impulses to earn bread and compete, both of which often leave them ambivalent about their obligations as fathers.

George Ingram, 48, lives on Capitol Hill with his sons Mason, 15, and Andrew, 10. He is the first to admit that single fatherhood has not helped his career as a political economist. "We're torn between working hard to become Secretary of State and nurturing our kids," he says. "You make the choice to nurture your kids, and people think it's great. But does it put a crimp on your career? Yes, very definitely. When I finish this process, I will have spent 15 years on a professional plateau." Ingram finds that his colleagues accept his dual commitments, his leaving every night before 6, or by 5 if he has a soccer practice to coach. In fact they are more accepting of his choices than those of his female colleagues. "I get more psychic support than women do," he says. "And I feel great about spending more time with my kids than my father did."

Maternal Gatekeepers

The more surprising obstacle, men say, arises in their own homes. Every household may be different, every division of labor unique, but sociologists do find certain patterns emerging when they interview groups of men and women about how they view one another's parenting roles. Men talk about their wife's unrealistic expectations, her perfectionism, the insistence on dressing, feeding, soothing the children in a certain way. "Fathers, except in rare circumstances, have not yet become equal partners in parenthood," says Frank Furstenberg, professor of sociology at the University of Pennsylvania. "The restructuring of the father role requires support and encouragement from wives. Presumably, it is not abnormal for wives to be reluctant to give up maternal prerogatives."

Many men describe in frustration their wife's attitude that her way of doing things is the only way. "Dad is putting the baby to bed," says Levine. "He's holding his seven-month-old on his shoulders and walking around in circles. Mom comes in and says, 'She likes it better when you just lay her down on her stomach and rub her back.' Dad gets mad that Mom is undermining his way of doing things, which he thinks works perfectly well."

In most cases, it is still the mother who carries her child's life around in her head, keeping the mental daybook on who needs a lift to piano practice and who needs to get the poetry folder in on time. After examining much of the research on men's housework and child care, Sylvia Hewlett concluded that married men's average time in household tasks had increased only 6% in 20 years, even as women have flooded the workplace. Psychologists Rosalind Barnett and Grace Baruch found that fathers were often willing to perform the jobs they were assigned but were not responsible for remembering, planning or scheduling them.

Women often respond that until men prove themselves dependable as parents, they can't expect to be trusted. A haphazard approach to family responsibilities does nothing to relieve the burdens women carry. "Men haven't been socialized to think about family appointments and how the household runs for kids," notes Marie Wilson of the Ms. Foundation for Women, who constantly hears of the hunger women feel for their husbands to participate more fully at home. "They don't really get in there and pay attention. Mothers often aren't sure they can trust them—not just to do it as they do it, but to do it at a level that you can get away with without feeling guilty."

Some women admit that their own feelings are mixed when it comes to relinquishing power within the family. "I can probably be overbearing at times as far as wanting to have it my way," says the 35-year-old wife of a St. Louis, Missouri, physician. "But I would be willing to relax my standards if he would be more involved. It would be a good trade-off." Here again the attitude is changing with each generation. Women under 35, researchers find, seem more willing than older women, whose own fathers were probably less engaged, to trust men as parents. Also, as younger women become more successful professionally, they are less fearful of relinquishing power at home because their identity and satisfaction come from many sources.

The New Father

The redefinition of fatherhood has been going on in virtually every arena of American life for well over 20 years. As women worked to broaden their choices at home and work, the implicit invitation was for men to do likewise. As Levine has observed, Dr. Spock had carefully revised his advice on fathers by 1974. The earlier version suggested that fathers change the occasional diaper and cautioned mothers about "trying to force the participation of fathers who get gooseflesh at the very idea of helping to take care of a baby." The new version of *Baby and Child Care,* by contrast, offered a prescription for the New Fatherhood: "The father—any father—should be sharing with the mother the day-to-day care of their child from birth onward . . . This is the natural way for the father to start the relationship, just as it is for the mother."

By the '80s, bookstores were growing fat with titles aimed at men: *How to Father, Expectant Father, Pregnant Fathers, The Birth of a Father, Fathers Almanac* and *Father Power.* There were books about child-and-father relations, like *How to Father a Successful Daughter,* and then specific texts for part-time fathers, single fathers, step-fathers and homosexual fathers. Bill Cosby's *Fatherhood* was one of the best-selling books in publishing history, and *Good Morning, Merry Sunshine,* by Chicago *Tribune* columnist Bob Greene, a journal about his first year of fatherhood, was on the New York *Times* best-seller list for almost a year. Parents can now pick up *Parents' Sports,* a new magazine dedicated to reaching the dad market with stories on the joys of soccer practice.

Institutions were changing too. In his book, *Fatherhood in America,* published this month, Robert L. Griswold has traced the history of a fast-changing role that today not only allows men in the birthing room (90% of fathers are in attendance at their child's birth) but also offers them postpartum courses in which new fathers learn how to change, feed, hold and generally take care of their infant. Some fathers may even get in on the pregnancy part by wearing the "empathy belly," a bulge the size and weight of a third-trimester fetus. Suddenly available to men hoping to solidify the father-child bond are "Saturday with Daddy Outings," special songfests, field trips and potlucks with dads. Even men behind bars could get help: one program allows an inmate father to read children's stories onto cassette tapes that are then sent, along with the book and a Polaroid picture of Dad, to his child.

"It's become cool to be a dad," says Wyatt Andrews, a correspondent for CBS News who has three children: Rachel, 8, Averil, 7, and Conrad, 5. "Even at dinner parties, disciplinary techniques are discussed. Fathers with teenagers give advice about strategies to fathers with younger kids. My father was career Navy. I don't think he ever spent two seconds thinking about strategies of child rearing. If he said anything, it was, 'They listen to me.'"

Bring Back Dad

These perceptual and behavioral shifts have achieved enough momentum to trigger a backlash of their own. Critics of the New

Fatherhood are concerned that something precious is being lost in the revolution in parenting—some uniquely male contribution that is essential for raising healthy kids. In a clinical argument that sends off political steam, these researchers argue that fathers should be more than substitute mothers, that men parent differently than women and in ways that matter enormously. They say a mother's love is unconditional, a father's love is more qualified, more tied to performance; mothers are worried about the infant's survival, fathers about future success. "In other words, a father produces not just children but socially viable children," says Blankenhorn. "Fathers, more than mothers, are haunted by the fear that their children will turn out to be bums, largely because a father understands that his child's character is, in some sense, a measure of his character as well."

When it comes to discipline, according to this school of thought, it is the combination of mother and father that yields justice tempered by mercy. "Mothers discipline children on a moment-by-moment basis," says Shapiro. "They have this emotional umbilical cord that lets them read the child. Fathers discipline by rules. Kids learn from their moms how to be aware of their emotional side. From dad, they learn how to live in society."

As parents, some psychologists argue, men and women are suited for different roles at different times. The image of the New Fatherhood is Jack Nicholson surrounded by babies on the cover of *Vanity Fair*, the businessman changing a diaper on the newly installed changing tables in an airport men's room. But to focus only on infant care misses the larger point. "Parenting of young infants is not a natural activity for males," says David Popenoe, an associate dean of social studies at Rutgers University who specializes in the family. He and others argue that women's voices are more soothing; they are better able to read the signals a child sends before he or she can talk. But as time passes, the strengths that fathers may bring to child rearing become more important.

"At a time when fatherhood is collapsing in our society," warns Blankenhorn, "when more children than ever in history are being voluntarily abandoned by their fathers, the only thing we can think of talking about is infant care? It's an anemic, adult-centered way of looking at the problem." Why not let mothers, he says, do more of the heavy lifting in the early years and let fathers do more of the heavy lifting after infancy when their special skills have more relevance? As children get older, notes William Maddox, director of research and policy at the Washington-based

Family Research Council, fathers become crucial in their physical and psychological development. "Go to a park and watch father and mother next to a child on a jungle gym," he said. "The father encourages the kid to challenge himself by climbing to the top; the mother tells him to be careful. What's most important is to have the balance of encouragement along with a warning."

This notion that men and women are genetically, or even culturally, predisposed to different parenting roles strikes other researchers as misguided. They are quick to reject the idea that there is some link between X or Y chromosomes and, say, conditional or unconditional love. "To take something that is only a statistical tendency," says historian E. Anthony Rotundo, "and turn it into a cultural imperative—fathers must do it this way and mothers must do it that way—only creates problems for the vast number of people who don't fit those tendencies, without benefiting the children at all." While researchers have found that children whose fathers are involved in their early rearing tend to have higher IQs, perform better in school and even have a better sense of humor, psychologists are quick to say this is not necessarily a gender issue. "It has to do with the fact that there are two people passionately in love with a child," says Harvard's Brazelton.

The very fact that psychologists are arguing about the nature of fatherhood, that filmmakers are making movies based entirely on fatherlove, that bookstores see a growth market in father guides speaks not only to children's well-being but to men's as well. As much as families need fathers, men need their children in ways they are finally allowed to acknowledge, to learn from them all the secrets that children, with their untidy minds and unflagging hearts, have mastered and that grownups, having grown up, long to retrieve.

ENDANGERED FAMILY[4]

Late on a sultry summer morning, Dianne Caballero settles onto her porch in the New York suburb of Roosevelt, bemused by the scene playing out across the street. Behind electric clippers, a

[4]Article by Michelle Ingrassia. From *Newsweek* 122(9):16–27 Ag 30 '93. Copyright © 1993 by Newsweek, Inc. Reprinted with permission.

muscular black man is trimming hedges with the intensity of a barber sculpting a fade; nearby, his wife empties groceries from the car. In most quarters, they might elicit barely a nod. But in this largely black, working-class community, the couple is one of the few intact families on the block. All too common are the five young women who suddenly turn into view, every one of them pushing a baby stroller, not one of them married. Resigned, Caballero says with a sigh. "Where are the men?"

It's a lament she knows too well. Like her mother before her and her daughter after, Caballero, who is black, had a child out of wedlock at 16. Twenty-three years later, even she is astounded at the gulf between motherhood and marriage. When her mother got pregnant in the '50s, she says, she was considered unique. When Caballero had a baby in 1970, no one ostracized her, though it still wasn't something "nice" girls did. But by the time her daughter had a baby seven years ago, it was regarded as "normal." Now, Caballero says regretfully, it's commonplace. "And there doesn't seem to be anything happening to reverse it."

That prospect troubles black leaders and parents alike, those like Caballero, who worries that her granddaughter is destined to be the fourth generation in her family to raise a child without a man. The odds are perilously high.

• For blacks, the institution of marriage has been devastated in the last generation: 2 out of 3 first births to black women under 35 are now out of wedlock. In 1960, the number was 2 out of 5. And it's not likely to improve any time soon. A black child born today has only a 1-in-5 chance of growing up with two parents until the age of 16, according to University of Wisconsin demographer Larry L. Bumpass. The impact, of course, is not only on black families but on all of society. Fatherless homes boost crime rates, lower educational attainment and add dramatically to the welfare rolls.

• Many black leaders rush to portray out-of-wedlock births as solely a problem of an entrenched underclass. It's not. It cuts across economic lines. Among the poor, a staggering 65 percent of never-married black women have children, double the number for whites. But even among the well-to-do, the differences are striking: 22 percent of never-married black women with incomes above $75,000 have children, almost 10 times as many as whites.

Nearly 30 years ago, Daniel Patrick Moynihan, then an assistant secretary of labor, caused a firestorm by declaring that fatherless homes were "the fundamental source of the weakness of the Negro Community." At the time, one quarter of black families were headed by women. Today the situation has only grown worse. A majority of black families with children—62 percent— are now headed by one parent. The result is what Johns Hopkins University sociologist Andrew Cherlin calls "an almost complete separation of marriage and childbearing among African-Americans."

It was not always so. Before 1950, black and white marriage patterns looked remarkably similar. And while black marriage rates have precipitously dipped since then, the desire to marry remains potent: a *Newsweek* Poll of single African-American adults showed that 88 percent said that they wanted to get married. But the dream of marriage has been hammered in the last 25 years. The economic dislocations that began in the '70s, when the nation shifted from an industrial to a service base, were particularly devastating to black men, who had migrated north in vast numbers to manufacturing jobs. The civil-rights movement may have ended legal segregation, but it hasn't erased discrimination in the work force and in everyday life. "When men lose their ability to earn bread, their sense of self declines dramatically. They lose rapport with their children," says University of Oklahoma historian Robert Griswold, author of "Fatherhood in America."

Some whites overlooked jobs and discrimination as factors in the breakdown of the black family. Back in the '60s, at the peak of the battle over civil rights, Moynihan infuriated blacks by describing a pattern of "pathology." Understandably, blacks were not willing to tolerate a public discussion that implied they were different—less deserving—than whites. The debate quickly turned bitter and polarized between black and white, liberal and conservative. Emboldened by a cultural sea change during the Reagan-Bush era, conservatives scolded, "It's all your fault." Dismissively, this camp insisted that what blacks need are mainstream American values—read: *white* values. Go to school, get a job, get married, they exhorted, and the family will be just fine. Not so, liberals fired back. As neoliberal University of Chicago sociologist William Julius Wilson argued in "The Declining Significance of Race," the breakdown of the African-American family resulted from rising unemployment, not falling values. Liberals have regarded the conservative posture as "blaming the victim," a phrase that, not coincidentally, white psychologist William Ryan coined in a 1965 assessment of Moynihan's study. To this camp, any family structure is good, as long as it's nurturing. "Marriage is important in the black community, just not the most important thing," says Andrew Billingsley, the University of Maryland sociologist who wrote the pioneering "Black Families in White America." "It is not an imperative for black people who can afford it."

Who's right? Both sides are too busy pointing fingers to find out. "We're never going to get to where we need to be if we first have to settle whose fault it is," says writer Nicholas Lemann, whose 1991 book, "The Promised Land," chronicles the great migration of blacks from the rural South to the industrialized North. But if there is any optimism, it is that now, after more than two decades on the defensive and with a Democratic president in the White House for the first time in 12 years, the African-American community is beginning to talk a little more openly about its problems. "Because of all the debate about morality, social programs, individual responsibility, it became very difficult to have an honest discussion," says Angela Glover Blackwell, who heads the Children's Defense Fund's Black Community Crusade for Children. "I'd like to think we've entered an era where we're willing to accept that there is a dual responsibility" between government and ordinary citizens.

Without question, government must do more to help. But increasingly, African-Americans are unwilling to wait for White America to step in. "During integration," says Virginia Walden, who owns a day-care center in Washington, D.C., "we kept saying that the white people did us wrong, and that they owed us. Well, white people did us wrong, but I tell my children, 'Don't nobody owe you anything. You've got to work for what you get.'" In response, many African-American men and women have thrown themselves into a range of grass-roots efforts from volunteer work in their communities to adopting children—stopgap efforts, perhaps, but to many, also cathartic and energizing. In many neighborhoods, the black church has led the awakening. Ministers began chastising themselves for sidestepping some basic moral issues. "We don't use 'family values' as an ax," says Wallace Smith, pastor of Shiloh Baptist Church in Washington. "But if someone is shacked up, we encourage them to get married." Smith is remarkably blunt about his own belief in the importance of a stable marriage. "Dan Quayle," he says, "was right."

At their kitchen tables and in their church basements every day, black families talk to each other, as they always have, about their fears. And part of what worries them is the growing tension between black men and black women, who are quick to blame each other for the massive retreat from marriage. "Black men say black women are 'Sapphires,' trying to dominate," explains Harvard psychologist Alvin Poussaint, referring to the wife of Kingfish in "Amos 'n' Andy," who epitomized the bitchy, bossy black woman. But Boston anchorwoman Liz Walker believes that many black men mistake self-reliance for highhandedness. "I don't think black women have thrown black men out," says Walker, who sparked a controversy when she became pregnant out of wedlock six years ago, long before TV's Murphy Brown knew what a home pregnancy test was. "I think black women have been abandoned."

More commonly, though, black women feel the fallout of the economic and psychological battering the African-American male has taken in the last generation. Of course black women want love and commitment. But not with a man whose chief qualification for marriage is that he's, well, a man. The remarkable success of Terry McMillan's 1991 novel, "Waiting to Exhale," underscores that passion. The book's main characters are four strong-minded black women who can't seem to find men who measure up. They clearly struck a nerve. "When Terry McMillan wrote that book, the reason it was so popular was because it was *us*," says Walker, 42. Giddy one night from too much birthday champagne and pepperoni pizza, McMillan's quartet—Robin, Gloria, Bernadine and Savannah—get to the essential question: what's happened to all the men, they ask. Where are they hiding?

They're ugly.
Stupid.
In prison.
Unemployed.
Crackheads.
Short.
Liars.
Unreliable.
Irresponsible.
Too possessive . . .
Childish.
Too goddamn old and set in their ways.

The litany drives the women to tears. But does marriage really matter? Or is a family headed by a single mother just as good as the nuclear unit? The evidence comes down solidly on the side of marriage. By every measure—economic, social, educational—the statistics conclude that two parents living together are better than one. Children of single mothers are significantly more likely to live in poverty than children living with both parents. In 1990, Census figures show, 65 percent of children of black single mothers were poor, compared with only 18 percent of children of black married couples. Educationally, children in one-parent homes are at greater risk across the board—for learning problems, for being left back, for dropping out. Psychiatrist James P. Comer, who teaches at Yale University's Child Study Center, says that the exploding population of African-American children from single-parent homes represents "the education crisis that is going to kill us. The crisis that we're concerned about—that Amerian kids don't achieve as well as European kids and some Asian kids— won't kill us because [the American students are] scoring high enough to compete. The one that will kill us is the large number of bright kids who fall out of the mainstream because their families are not functioning."

Statistics tell only part of the story. Equally important are the intangibles of belonging to an intact family. "Growing up in a married family is where you learn the value of the commitments you make to each other, rather than seeing broken promises," says Roderick Harrison, chief of the Census Bureau's race division. "It deals with the very question of what kind of personal commitments people can take seriously."

Boys in particular need male role models. Without a father, who will help them define what it means to be a man? Fathers do things for their children that mothers often don't. Though there are obviously exceptions, fathers typically encourage independence and a sense of adventure, while mothers are more nurturing and protective. It is men who teach boys how to be fathers. "A woman can only nourish the black male child to a certain point," says Bob Crowder, an Atlanta lawyer and father of four, who helped organize an informal support group for African-American fathers. "And then it takes a man to raise a boy into a man. I mean a real man." Mothers often win the job by default, and struggle to meet the challenge. But sometimes, even a well-intentioned single mother can be smothering, especially if her son is the only man in her life. Down the road a few years, she hears erstwhile daughters-in-law lament how she "ruined" him for every other woman. Like the street-smart New Yorker she is, Bisi Ruckett, who is Dianne Caballero's daughter, says flat out that she can't "rule" her boyfriend. And just as quickly, she concedes she can't compete with his mom. "If he tells her he needs a zillion dollars, she'll get it," says Ruckett, 23.

Without a father for a role model, many boys learn about relationships from their peers on the street. In the inner city in particular, that often means gangs; and the message they're selling is that women are whores and handmaidens, not equals. Having a father does not, of course, guarantee that the lessons a young male learns will be wholesome. But research shows that, with no father, no minister, no boss to help define responsibility, there's nothing to prevent a boy from treating relationships perversely. University of Pennsylvania professor Elijah Anderson, who authored a 1990 study on street life, says that, among the poor, boys view courting as a "game" in which the object is to perfect a rap that seduces girls. The goal: to add up one's sexual conquests, since that's the measure of "respect."

Often, for a girl, Anderson says, life revolves around the "dream," a variation on the TV soaps in which a man will whisk her away to a life of middle-class bliss—even though everywhere she looks there are only single mothers abandoned by their boyfriends. Not surprisingly, the two sexes often collide. The girl dreams because she must. "It has to do with one's conception of oneself: 'I will prevail'," Anderson says. But the boy tramples that dream because he must—his game is central to his vision of respect. "One of the reasons why, when a woman agrees to have a baby, these men think it's such a victory is that you have to get her to go against all the stuff that says he won't stick around."

For teenage mothers not mature enough to cope, single parenthood is not the route to the dream, but entrapment. They have too many frustrations: the job, the lack of a job, the absence of a man, the feeling of being dependent on others for help, the urge to go out and dance instead of pacing with a crying child. Taken to its extreme, says Poussaint, the results can be abuse or neglect. "They'll see a child as a piece of property or compete with the child—calling them dumb or stupid, damaging their growth and education to maintain superiority," he says. The middle class is not exempt from such pain. Even with all the cushions money could buy—doctors and backup doctors, nannies and backup nannies—Liz Walker says that trying to raise her son, Nicholas, alone was draining. "Certainly, the best situation is to have as many people in charge of a family as possible," says Walker, who is now married to Harry Graham, a 41-year-old corporate-tax lawyer; together, they're raising her son and his two children from a previous marriage. "I can see that now," she adds. "Physically, you *need* it."

More and more, black men aren't there to build marriages or to stick around through the hard years of parenting. The question we're too afraid to confront is why. The biggest culprit is an economy that has locked them out of the mainstream through a pattern of bias and a history of glass ceilings. "The economic state of the African-American community is worse in 1993 than it was in 1963," says NAACP head Benjamin Chavis Jr. He could be speaking, just as easily, about the black family, since the two fell in tandem.

A man can't commit to a family without economic security, but for many African-American men, there is none. The seeds of modern economic instability date back to the 1940s, when the first of $6\frac{1}{2}$ million blacks began migrating from the rural South to the urban North as farm mechanization replaced the need for their backs and hands. At first, black men built a solid economic niche by getting factory jobs. But just as the great migration ended in the '70s, the once limitless industrial base began to cave in. And as steel mills and factories swept offshore, the "last hired, first fired" seniority rules disproportionately pushed black men out. During that time, says Billingsley, unemployment for blacks became twice as high as it was for whites, "and it has rarely dropped below that [ratio] since." Unarguably, economic restructuring hit whites as well as blacks, but the new service sector favored those with education—and there were many more educated white men than blacks in the '70s as vast numbers of baby boomers streamed out of the nation's colleges looking for jobs.

Ironically, just as the job market collapsed for black men, it opened for black women, who went to college while black men went to war. Armed with the college degrees that black males didn't have and pushed by the burgeoning women's movement, growing numbers of black women found spots in corporate America. As with white women in the '80s, that bought them greater independence. But the jobs of black women came at the expense of black men. Throughout the workplace, says Yale's Comer, "there was a trade-off. The one black woman was a two-fer: you got a black and a woman." Since then, the gap between white women's income and black women's has disappeared—black women's salaries are the same as whites'.

But the chasm between black and white men has barely moved. In 1969, black men earned 61 cents for every dollar white men earned; by 1989, the number had increased to only 69 cents. And that's for black men who were working; more and more, they

found themselves without jobs. During the same time, the number of black men with less than a high-school education who
found jobs dropped from two thirds to barely half. And it's likely
to worsen: in the last 25 years, the proportion of black men in
college has steadily eroded. "America has less use for black men
today than it did during slavery," says Eugene Rivers, who helps
run computer-training programs as pastor of Boston's Azusa
Christian Community.

Though he is scarcely 11, Lugman Kolade dreams of becoming an electrical engineer. But he already wears the grievous pain
of a man who feels left out. Lugman is a small, studious, Roman
Catholic schooler from Washington, D.C., who will enter the sixth
grade this fall, a superb student who won the archdiocese science
fair with a homemade electric meter. Unlike most boys in the
Male Youth Project he attended at Shiloh Baptist Church, his
parents are married. His mother works for the Department of
Public Works; describing what his father does doesn't come easy.
"My father used to be a [construction] engineer. He left his job
because they weren't treating him right; they would give white
men better jobs who did less work. Now he drives an ice-cream
truck."

Black men were hurt, too, by the illegal economy. As the legitimate marketplace cast them aside, the drug trade took off, enlist-
ing anyone lured by the promise of fast money. Ironically, says
Comer, "you had to make a supreme and extra effort to get into
the legal system and no effort to get into the illegal system." For
many on the fringes, there was no contest. "It overwhelmed the
constructive forces in the black mainstream," he says. Disproportionately, too, black men are in prison or dead. While African-
Americans represent only 12 percent of the population, they
composed 44 percent of the inmates in state prisons and local jails
in 1991; and, in 1990, homicide was the leading cause of death
for young black men.

The economy explains only one part of what happened. The
sexual revolution in the '70s was the second great shift that
changed the black family. Although the social tide that erased
taboos against unwed motherhood affected all women, whites
and blacks took different paths. White women delayed both marriage and childbearing, confident that, down the road, there
would be a pool of marriageable men. Not so for black women,
who delayed marriage but not children because they were less
certain there would be men for them. In what they called a "strik-

ing shift," Census officials reported earlier this year that less than 75 percent of black women are likely to ever marry, compared with 90 percent of whites.

More dramatic is the childbearing picture. Between 1960 and 1989, the proportion of young white women giving birth out of wedlock rose from 9 to 22 percent, markedly faster than it did for blacks. The slower rate of increase for blacks was small comfort. Their rate—42 percent—was already so high by 1960 that if it had kept pace with the white rate, it would have topped 100 percent by now. As things stand, it's 70 percent.

Traditionally, the extended family has served as a safety net. But the terrible irony of history is that it has also hurt the black family. While intended as a cushion, the network, in effect, enabled more single women to have children. And that helps explain why not only poor black women, but middle- and upper-class blacks as well, have had children out of wedlock at higher rates than white women. Historically, white women have had only themselves to rely on for child rearing, and so marriage became more of an imperative. For blacks, the network of extended kin is a tradition rooted in African customs that emphasize community over marriage. Although historians say that most black children grew up in two-parent households during slavery, as well as in the 19th and early 20th centuries, high rates of poverty, widowhood and urban migration reinforced the need for interdependence that continues today. The oft-repeated African proverb "It takes a whole village to raise a child" echoes back to that.

Now the extended family is breaking down. Yet the black family's expectations for it haven't diminished. Both sides feel the strains. With the soaring number of teenage mothers, grandparents today are getting younger and more likely to be working themselves. A 32-year-old grandmother isn't necessarily eager, or able, to raise a grandchild, especially when that child becomes a teenager and the problems multiply. And, after generations of no fathers, there are no grandfathers, either. What's more, the tradition of a real neighborhood is disappearing. "It used to be that everyone looked out for everyone else," said community activist Claudette Burroughs-White of Greensboro, N.C. "Now I think people are kind of estranged. They don't get involved. It's safer not to." Many families left in the inner city—the ones most in need of support—are increasingly isolated from relatives able to flee to the suburbs. "Not every poor black mother is in a strong kinship network," says Cherlin. "Many are living alone, hiding behind double-locked doors in housing projects."

What's the solution? Nearly 30 years after Lyndon Johnson launched the War on Poverty, experts on the black family return again and again to the same ideas—better education, more jobs, discouraging teen pregnancy, more mentoring programs. But now the question is, who should deliver—government or blacks themselves? Ever since the government started abandoning social programs in the '70s and early '80s, black families have been left on their own to find a way out. Those who would argue against funneling in more government dollars say we tried that, but "nothing works." Lemann, who believes that most of the positive social changes in Black America were sparked by government intervention, dismisses the conceit that spending on social welfare failed. The War on Poverty, he says, "threw out some untested ideas, some of which worked"—like Head Start, the Job Corps and Foster Grandparents—"and some of which didn't." Beyond the all-or-nothing extremes, there is room for solutions. Moynihan believes the nation has been in a collective "denial phase" about the black family for the last 25 years. But he says he's encouraged. "We're beginning to get a useful debate on this."

Will self-help do it? Though few African-American leaders expect what they call "White America" to come to the rescue, they're equally skeptical that the thousands of programs filling church rec rooms and town-hall meeting rooms can, on their own, turn things around. "People who are trying to salvage a lot of the children are burnt out, they think it's like spitting into the ocean," says Poussaint, who doesn't dispute the pessimism. "The real problems are overwhelming. It's like treating lung cancer and knowing that people are still smoking."

There aren't many places left to look for answers. When black leaders speak with one voice, it is about the deep crisis of faith and purpose that came with integration: the very promise that African-Americans would be brought into the American mainstream has left many by the wayside. What's the penalty for doing nothing? "We could revert to a caste society," says Moynihan. Others are just as bleak. There are sparks of hope, says Comer, but he warns: "It's getting late, very late." The problems of the black family have been apparent for decades. And so has our collective understanding that we must take them on. What we need to find now is a voice to start the dialogue.

II. THE CHILD-CARE CRISIS

EDITOR'S INTRODUCTION

In 1993 Americans welcomed a new generation into the White House and into the top ranks of the federal government. When two of President Clinton's candidates for Attorney General withdrew because neither one of them paid social security taxes for their baby-sitters, the needs, wants and desires of a whole new elite became the stuff of popular discussion. If Zoë Baird and Kimba Wood did not hire legal sitters on their salaries, what are the rest of us doing?

The child-care system in the United States has been described as chaotic. It is a patchwork of center-based care, in-home care, and neighborhood "family-based" care. Many observers have suggested that the disorganized nature of the system can be blamed on a continuing cultural uneasiness with child care. For this reason, the movement of women into the labor market is an unfinished revolution, because the position of women in the work force will not be stabilized until there is a more uniform system of child care that addresses the issues of quality, affordability, and availability.

The first article in this section, "Save the Children," by Catherine Johnson, provides a vivid picture of working women who are caught between their own needs and the needs of their children. Dr. Johnson describes the problems that exist within the child-care industry and suggests that we should rethink how it is being used. Is reaching the top of your profession, at the expense of time with your children, the true test of human value? Dr. Johnson concludes that parents need to seek greater work week flexibility and corporations must recognize and support family priorities.

The following article, "Child-Care Quagmire," from *National Journal*, looks at child care as a political issue. There is considerable opportunity available with a new administration to look at new solutions to child-care problems. Tax reform, welfare reform and regulatory reform are currently being discussed. It is important to understand that tax credits do not offer much help to lower-income parents who have little or no tax liability. Subsidies for day care exist in a confusing array of programs, paying amounts that are not high enough to assure quality care. *Head Start* is very successful, but it is not meant to be child-care and only runs on a half-day schedule and only during the school year. Should it become a full-time, year-round program?

The third article in this section, "Mary Poppins Speaks Out," by Melinda Beck, examines the conditions in the child-care industry. The article reflects on how those who utilize in-home child-care treat those who care for their children. If the inequalities of the feminist movement are going to be redressed, domestic workers need to be treated like any others and be paid an on-the-books, living wage.

The fourth article in this section, "Nannygate for the Poor," reprinted from the *New York Times*, describes the widespread underground economy of unlicensed care-givers. There are many unlicensed care-givers who have outstanding local reputations, but have chosen not to become licensed because of the complications. Parents must make some very difficult choices. Without widespread child-care subsidies, some people are forced to make a choice between unlicensed care for their children and welfare.

The final article in this section, "Enforcing Child Care Standards," by Penny R. Thompson, is a careful analysis of the problems of federally standardized child-care. Currently, child care is regulated on the state and local level. Some federal regulations have been tied to federal funding initiatives, but enforcement is uneven. In this era of shrinking state and municipal budgets where is the money for federal, child-care inspector's salaries going to come from? It is very hard to regulate some of the intangible qualities that make someone an effective care-giver.

SAVE THE CHILDREN[1]

I was brought up in the 1950s, when almost no one's mother worked outside the home—no one who was middle-class, that is. And the fates of the children whose mothers did work seemed

[1]Article by Catherine Johnson. From *New Woman* 22(2):60–65 F '92. Copyright © 1992. Reprinted with permission of the author.

only to reinforce people's feelings that a woman's place was in the home. I remember the sole businesswoman in our neighborhood (she oversaw her husband's thriving car dealership); I remember what happened to her children. By age 16 both girls were pregnant and out of school; the boy was to suffer a serious mental breakdown in his late 20s. In those days no one had any doubt that the problem was an absent mother. She should have been home, people thought; her children needed her.

Today, of course, we know better than to blame their fate on their mom's absence. Thanks, in part, to a new emphasis on genetics, biology, and on psychosocial influences, mothers are no longer held completely accountable for everything that happens to their children. And, at the same time, the politics of women working has changed so much that many of us now believe that the working mom is actually the better mom. A mother who feels fulfilled in her adult world of work, many people think, will feel happier and be better to her children than the mother who stays home frustrated and alone.

So, today we wouldn't blame my neighbor for her children's problems. We might see the son's breakdown as the result of an inherited biochemical imbalance, the daughter's teenage pregnancies as the result of a conservative small-town attitude that calls for withholding birth control from the young.

Still, as a working mother myself, I cannot help but be haunted by the image of those three children with whom I grew up; I cannot help but think of how my working hours away from my young son might affect who he is to become. I know I am not alone in my thoughts. Many working mothers worry about how their careers will affect their children's welfare and happiness.

Perhaps we worry, in part, because no one actually *knows* that having our children spend large portions of their childhood in day care is a good thing. If we are honest with ourselves we can't help but look at our culture and see a massive, real-life, social-science experiment being conducted in the rearing of our small sons and daughters. Between 1970 and 1988 the proportion of mothers with children under age 6 who went back to work rose from 30 to 56 percent, and in 1987 more than one half of all mothers of babies 1 year or younger were either working or looking for work. In families in which both parents now work, we have doubled the family workweek from 40 hours to 80 hours—even to 90-plus when you count commuting, overtime, and, for some, a longer workweek.

Judging by public opinion surveys, many of us have our doubts as to whether everything is going to be all right for our children. Recently the *Los Angeles Times* conducted a poll of southern California parents, finding that 80 percent of mothers and 40 percent of fathers in Los Angeles and Orange counties say they would leave their jobs if they could to raise their children at home. In 1990, pollsters for Virginia Slims found that half of all women surveyed across the nation believe that the ideal maternity leave would last at least until a child is 2 years old. Thirty-two percent say that (again, in an ideal world) a working woman should stay at home with her children until they entered school. Only 5 percent of respondents thought six weeks an ideal maternity leave. At the same time, few women actually wanted to stay home during their children's preschool years: only 6 percent said that leaving work would make *their* lives better. Working mothers appeared to be living in a state of conflict. What was good for children, they seemed to be saying, was not necessarily good for mothers.

All these people seem to know something: that families are nearing a breaking point. And chances are they fear for our nation's children, who seem to be at risk on every front. Consider this catalog of bleak statistics as to how our children are turning out: only 71 percent of our teenagers graduate from high school as compared with 95 percent in Japan; S.A.T. scores have dropped 60 points since 1969; one study of single-parent families found that 49 percent of the children had not seen their nonresident parent for a year. Many children spend a significant amount of time at home in the absence of *either* parent: in 1987, 25 percent of 11- to 13-year-olds and 5 percent of 5- to 7-year-olds were home alone for periods ranging from one hour a week to 20. Statistics on suicide are also troubling: in 1990, 27.3 percent of all students in grades 9 through 12 had thought seriously about suicide; and the actual suicide rates for this age group have quadrupled in the last 40 years.

The economics of the Reagan era also pushed more families into poverty and robbed many families of the "luxury" of a full-time parent in the home. As a result, time for children has shrunk dramatically as both parents go to work to try to supply their children with the lifestyle that their own parents were able to give them on one income alone.

Particularly in urban America, there are some children who wear $40 blue jeans, attend $6,000-a-year private elementary schools, and are cared for by nannies while their parents put in the extra hours required by their high-powered professions. And small wonder, since for the past ten years our generation has been bombarded with the message that working long hours in order to reach the *top* is the true test of our worth as human beings.

Now, some of us are beginning to rethink this definition of success. Some of us are beginning to say that time with our children is just as valuable—and just as deserving of respect as time with clients and colleagues.

The Time Crunch. Pollster Lou Harris estimates that, overall, the average American workweek increased from 40.6 hours in 1973 to 48.8 hours in 1985. Clearly, some professionals see their children only at bedtime, if then. And, for many the family meal no longer exists.

The fact is, two jobs in one family means that (in the best of all possible scenarios) on weekdays the child spends eight hours at day care and only three to four waking hours at home. The notion of "quality time," not often heard on the lips of real-life working parents, is at the very best wildly unrealistic; it is not as if work stops once mother and father arrive home. That is simply when the burden of the "second shift"—as Arlie Hochschild calls it in her book by that title—falls on most women. Weekends are spent on such tasks as running errands and cleaning the house.

And, of course, there is the time crunch faced by children whose parents have divorced. Between 1930 and 1970, roughly 90 percent of all children lived in intact families; now only 75 percent of children ages 6 to 17 live in homes with *both* parents present. The loss of quality time between parents and their children, even after the most amicable of divorces, is enormous.

The Money Crunch. Middle-class family life is enormously costly these days, just owning a small three-bedroom home is a major financial challenge in many parts of the country. Estimates of the cost of raising a child born today to age 17 range from a "low" of $150,000 to high of nearly $300,000 for parents in the highest-income levels—and the bill for college comes on top of that (a bill demographer Cheryl Russell projects will be an average of $30,000 a year for today's parents.)

Not only are costs rising but our expectations of what we should be *able* to provide for our children may have risen also. The 1980s was a period of near-total obsession with materialism and money, Wall Street, *Dynasty,* Donald Trump—it was the decade of greed. Everyone was judged according to her or his professional status.

Open your business magazines to the feature section and what do you see? Pictures of glamorous career women sitting posed and confident in their offices, looking svelte and unruffled in their finely tailored suits. In the media, there are no high-profile stay-at-home moms (or dads).

With such images presented as the ideal, not only is it difficult for a woman or a man to cut back on her or his career financially, it is very difficult psychologically as well. There is precious little social support for such choices; when people at parties ask what you do, "I'm a mother" (or, worse, "I'm a house husband") does not earn you points. The danger is that as we work harder to give our children enough materially, we may be necessarily forced to give them less and less intellectually and emotionally.

Rethinking Day Care. All of these contemporary pressures have sparked some parents to rebel in what might be called a "family liberation movement." Many parents are beginning to rethink their lives, to question the dominant work-oriented values of the day. This means rethinking children, career, and day care, and reexamining the image of the glamorous career woman who, juggling a job and two children, is presented as having it all. Her children, we're led to assume, never give their parents any trouble.

Anyone who has had children—especially anyone who has had more than one child—knows different. There *are* easy children in the world, the kind of precocious, cooperative, innately sociable little children who take to day care like fish to water do exist. But there are plenty of children who aren't "easy"—and you don't get to choose which kind you'll have.

Sarah Gilbert, a middle-level manager living in northern California, has been lucky in this respect. "Everyone tells me what an easy baby Lauren is, from her baby-sitter on up to strangers on the street," she says.

Everyone loves an easy child, and Lauren's day-care provider frequently compares Lauren favorably to a little boy who is also in her care. This little boy sobs inconsolably every morning when his mothers drops him off, a recurring scene that irritates his caretaker. She will tell Gilbert, in private, that this little boy is too clingy, fearful, and needy. That is all very well and good for Lauren who comes off as the shining star of day dare. But what is the caretaker's attitude doing for the little boy? Are her actions and attitudes toward him throughout the day colored by the impatience she feels with him each morning? In fact, shortly after

my interview with Gilbert, her daughter's caretaker decided to
drop the little boy who now faces the added challenge of starting
over again with a new caretaker.)

This little boy might seem like a special case. But most children have their problems, or at least their bad phases, and parents worry whether our nation's day-care workers (among the
lower-paid employees in the entire labor force) are up to the
challenges these special children, or special developmental phases,
require. To put it bluntly, how motivated to deal sensitively with a
Terrible Two (or a Terrible Three or a Terrible Four. . .)-year-
old is a caretaker being paid slave wages? In 1987 more than half
of all day-care providers were earning less than $5 per hour, and
every parent's fear is: What if we *are* getting what we pay for?

For a number of years now, psychologists and educators have
been asking this question. Several researchers have discovered
that children who enter day care during the first year of life are
more likely to show anxious-avoidant attachments to their mothers. And, after a thorough survey of the research literature on
day care, a panel from The National Academy of Sciences has
recommended that we, as a nation, find some way to make it
possible for one parent to be home full-time with a new baby
during its first year of life. But you have to wonder: if day care is
harmful during the first year of life, how does it suddenly become
benign once the baby turns 1?

The late British psychologist John Bowlby, developer of the
highly influential school of "attachment" theory, held that there
are "striking similarities between the way a child. . . responds to a
separation experience and the way an adult responds to bereave-
ment." In short: being separated from his mother for a significant
period of time is, to a baby, what death of a loved one is to an
adult? Psychoanalyst René Spitz's classic, and deeply saddening,
studies of small babies separated from their parents supported
Bowlby's contentions. Spitz's babies, placed in clean and well-
maintained institutions where all their nutritional needs are met,
failed to thrive. Many babies withdrew completely, refusing to
take part in life or their surroundings. Maternal deprivation
came to be seen as a very damaging form of abuse.

This was long before day care became an issue, but you can
see the connection: many very young children are now being left
in institutional settings for large portions of their day. While The
National Academy of Sciences has concluded that institutional
day care does *not* constitute "maternal deprivation," nonetheless

it is doubtful that most children in large centers are being treated with motherly attention and care for much of their day. Psychology professor Nancy McWilliams, Ph.D., of Rutgers University, comments: "The upsetting thing to me is that in very institutionalized day care, no one is loving up a child *personally*."

"Loving up" a child personally in a day-care center is difficult at best given the instability of the work force. The annual turnover rate for child-care workers is estimated to stand at 40 percent. And this figure is not likely to change unless our government backs us up with subsidies for higher pay. But given the deficit, the shaky state of the economy, and the high cost of paying for the recent war in the Persian Gulf, how do we devote more time, energy, and money to children and still maintain our standard of living? While we, as a nation, have just spent 50 years footing the bill for the Cold War, many other countries have been pouring much of their money into day care and education, leaving us far behind much of the Western world in terms of resources devoted to *children*.

In Sweden either parents is eligible to take a one-year *paid* leave after the birth or adoption of a baby. In France paid leave is much shorter, usually beginning six weeks before the birth and continuing for only ten weeks after delivery. During this period French Social Security pays the mother 90 percent of her salary. However, mothers (or fathers) employed by large firms are also guaranteed *two years* of unpaid leave. After spending two years at home with her baby, a French mother can return to work, secure in the knowledge that her position will be there for her. Her child, now age 2, can attend a publicly financed nursery school if she chooses.

Because France is concerned about a falling birth rate, the government has taken many steps to make parenthood as attractive as possible. French families also enjoy "family allowances"— money paid to support their children and pay for day care if both are working. While the American system views the having of children as a personal choice, with costs that must be born by the person making that choice, France sees childbearing as a productive activity that is good for the nation.

In short, the French, as a society, have made a major commitment to children—both to the children of working parents *and* to the children with a parent at home full-time. In the words of France's President François Mitterrand, "France will blossom in its children." And this past November, the *New York Times* report-

ed that all European Community nations agreed to guarantee
women 14 weeks maternity leave at wages at least equal to the sick
pay offered in their countries.

Meanwhile, in this country, the government is hoping that the
private sector will step in and worry about the future of our
children. But don't we need government to help us here? Just as
private businesses don't build roads or declare war, private businesses are not equipped to oversee the nation's family policy.
What we need is a government that will *govern,* passing laws to
support paid leaves, unpaid leaves, part-time jobs with health
benefits and nondiscriminatory promotion practices, and high-
quality day care for all. We need a government willing to pass
some type of family and medical leave act, such as the one vetoed
two summers ago by President Bush, which would have ruled that
all companies with 50 or more employees must offer workers up
to 12 weeks unpaid leave to care for a new child or to deal with
family health problems. And we need a government able to find a
way to come up with the money to do these things. Our families
need a peace dividend.

How Fathers Can Make the Difference

Although working mothers may continue to be less available
than mothers of decades past, if today's fathers become more
available, that will make up for some of the lost parenting time.
Ron Levant founded the Boston University Fatherhood Project
precisely for this reason; its mission: to teach men the crucial
parenting skills that were omitted from their education. "There
has been a change in fathers," he says. "Studies of men's attitudes
show that men now value family more than work. So their attitudes have changed, but their behavior hasn't altered all that
much." Levant also notes that the proportion of total "family
work" performed by men nationally only increased from 20 percent to 30 percent from 1965 to 1981, which is significant but still
leaves women doing 70 percent.

Changing Our View of Work

Changes need to occur in the workplace, too. To begin, we
desperately need to redefine the workweek. Why are the number
of hours we spend on the job increasing? Are employees actually
accomplishing more the longer they stay at the office?

Research into the nature of work says no. Psychologist Mihaly Csikszentmihalyi, Ph.D., reports in his recent book *Flow* that Americans spend only 30 hours a week actually working. The other hours are spent daydreaming, taking coffee breaks, making personal phone calls, and chatting with co-workers. In other words, one quarter of the day is spent on personal things.

This is precisely where the issues of flextime, part-time jobs, and on-site day care come in. A woman (or a man) who works at home can spend her or his 25 percent "downtime" with the children. Good on-site day care would allow parents who must travel to an office the same option. Flextime and part-time jobs achieve much the same goal: they encourage employees to spend their time at work *working*, with personal time given over to their children.

For these solutions truly to be solutions, of course, the business world must come to recognize, and support, an employee's commitment to family. Traditionally, of course, this has not been the case. In her book of ten years back, *Men and Woman of the Corporation*, Rosabeth Moss Kanter, Ph.D., revealed that corporations expect their managers to devote their entire lives to the business if they hope to advance. And in a more recent study, one high-level executive told researchers that he personally measured loyalty and performance by how many cars were in the parking lot on Saturdays.

Happily, this may already be changing. You know something new is afoot when a famous female journalist feels comfortable announcing to the public that she is drastically reducing her workload in order to "take a very aggressive approach to having a baby" (*aggressive* is a term doctors often use to describe intensive fertility treatments). Far from setting her back, Connie Chung's willingness to sacrifice work for a wished-for pregnancy landed her on the cover of *People* magazine. Chances are that when she returns to work she will resume a brilliant career. And she will have found a way to take time out for motherhood.

I think it is fair to hope for, and to ask for, a trickle-down effect, with the rights that are being given to highly successful women granted eventually to all women and men. But accompanying this change we also need to see a wider cultural change, a change in the social definition of success. It needs to be seen as okay to "plateau," okay and even admirable to slow down one's career in order to give more time to family. Alongside all those news photos of fast-track women, we need to see some equally appealing images of men and women who have pulled back a bit, men and women who aren't wearing the $1,000 business suits they earned by dint of an 80-hour workweek. Men and women who have made time for children and are reaping the quieter rewards.

CHILD CARE QUAGMIRE[2]

Denied the opportunity to go down in history as the nation's first female Attorney General, maybe Zoë E. Baird and Judge Kimba M. Wood will make the books as the working mothers who finally forced society to confront the issue of child care head-on.

"The silver lining in the Zoë Baird story is that for weeks I've been on the phone with the press," Marcy Whitebook, the director of the Oakland-based Child Care Employee Project, said in an interview. "I think that story is helping to break the silence about how bad the child care problem is and raise the awareness of the general public, the policy makers and media."

Several opportunities to deal with parts of the problem hover on the horizon. For starters, two priorities of the Clinton Administration—welfare reform and expansion of the $2.8 billion Head Start preschool program for poor children—could provide a forum for discussing the child care needs of low-income families.

As part of the economic plan that he unveiled to the nation on Feb. 17, President Clinton pledged to plow an additional $9.3 billion into Head Start by fiscal 1998. "Head Start is a success story," he said, "It saves money, but today it reaches only one-third of all eligible children. Under our plan we will cover every eligible child."

And a new round of tax reform this year could put on the agenda bigger tax subsidies for families that pay for child care. But that's just picking at pieces of the problem, say child care experts, who yearn for a wide-open national debate on the issue.

The nation's reluctance to look at child care as a legitimate need of families across the economic spectrum has stymied the development of a comprehensive and articulated menu of child

[2]Article by Rochelle L. Stanfield. From *National Journal* 25(9):512–516 F 27 '93. Copyright © 1993 by National Journal, Inc. Reprinted with permission.

care options, a step that many European countries have already taken.

"We have to come to see children who are under 5 years old in the same we see children over 5, as part of societal responsibility," Carla B. Howery, a child care specialist who is the deputy executive officer of the American Sociological Association in Washington, said in an interview.

For the poor, child care is frequently a prerequisite to getting off welfare and obtaining a decent job with full-time benefits. But child care subsidies come from more than a dozen programs with conflicting and confusing federal regulations that often drive recipients off the job and back onto welfare.

For middle-class parents, finding good, affordable child care is mostly a matter of luck and sufficient income, although the federal government helps a bit on the financial side. Parents can take a tax credit for child care if they meet certain requirements. Quality is an iffier proposition. State and local regulations, which are intended to control the quality of child care, often are lax and in some cases only drive the system underground.

Ultimately, the adequacy of the nation's child care system rests on the availability of qualified child care workers. But because the average pay is so low (it hovers around the poverty line), many experienced child care workers have been driven from the field.

Day care centers average about 40 per cent turnover a year, in fact, even though young children do much better in stable environments. Whitebook's most recent study, which followed day care workers over four years, found that at the end of the period, more than two-thirds had left their jobs.

Child care expert Deborah Phillips, a psychology professor at the University of Virginia who lives in Washington, summed up the issue from personal and professional perspectives. She and her husband, a congressional aide, send their 2-year-old son, Samuel, to the Senate Child Care Center, a highly regarded facility that's open to children of congressional and other government employees.

"I'm just very lucky to be able to afford [good child care] and to live somewhere that offers it," Phillips said in a recent interview. "That's the kind of care that should be universally available. People know that what we have in this country is a mess. And they are beginning to ask, 'How on earth do you begin to fix it?' What we really need to do is to step back and think very carefully about the needs of children and families, and then design a system around that."

A Sensitive Subject

Child Care remains a surprisingly touchy subject, a holdover of the 1950s-era notion that only mothers can properly care for their children.

Perhaps that's why child care emerged slowly and cautiously as a central theme of the Baird-Wood saga. Even Hillary Rodham Clinton, who made child care a high priority when she chaired the Washington-based Children's Defense Fund (CDF) in the 1980s, passed up a recent opportunity to highlight the issue. In an early-February interview, *Newsweek* asked Clinton whether the Administration's problems in finding an Attorney General "says anything about the day care situation in this country." She answered: "Probably, but I haven't analyzed that."

But *why* is the issue of child care such a sensitive subject? "Perhaps our [public] dialogue is very convoluted because of feelings we have about whether [child care] is appropriate," Helen Blank, CDF's director of child care, said in an interview. "It's important that we start to be honest about what the situation is and what we need to make the system work for families. The economy has changed and women have to work. That's not going to go away."

More than half the mothers of children less than year old work outside the home, according to the Bureau of Labor Statistics, as do nearly two-thirds of mothers of children age 3–5 and three-fourths of mothers of children ages 6–13. Mothers of infants constitute the most rapidly growing segment of the nation's work force.

In the past, many working mothers could leave their children with relatives or neighbors. But now, many of those handy substitute mothers are out working themselves. In 1977, only 13 per cent of children under 5 whose mothers worked outside the home went to group day care, according to a Census Bureau survey. By 1988, the proportion had doubled.

In the wake of the disclosures by Baird and Wood that they had employed illegal aliens as nannies, the nation's news media rushed out stories about the availability of legal nannies and the hassles of complying with federal tax and immigration laws. It looked like a universal problem. But only 3 per cent of all working mothers (about 900,000 families) rely on in-home child care, and only a small fraction of the care givers are live-in nannies, the federally sponsored 1990 National Child Care Survey reported.

No one knows for sure how many of those nannies are illegal aliens. But Jeffrey S. Passel, who researches immigration policy at the Washington-based Urban Institute, figures that fewer than 100,000 undocumented workers are engaged in child care. "It's just not a huge number," he said.

The overwhelming majority of families use some form of group day care, according to the 1990 survey, including about 80,000 licensed preschools, 118,000 regulated family day care centers (in the home of the provider) and as many as 1.1 million nonregulated day care centers.

But change seems inevitable. Through a combination of demographic and economic factors, mothers of young children have finally made it to the top rungs of government, professional and corporate ladders. They have money and more clout than ever before. They demand high-quality child care but have a hard time finding it. And finally, for the first time, they're in a position to do something about the problem.

Care for the Poor

Despite society's general reluctance to intervene in the lives of children under 5, the federal government has had few qualms about butting in when they are on welfare or merely poor.

"As a society, we're still ambivalent about the idea that women with young children should be at work," said Catherine W. Berheide, a sociology professor at Skidmore College in Saratoga Springs, N.Y. "Yet we feel that mothers who do not have other sources of income should be employed."

The government takes one approach in helping poor children and a radically different tack in supporting their parents. Not surprisingly, conflict and confusion result.

Head Start, the biggest and oldest child care program (it was launched in 1965), is aimed at the children. Although the goal is mainly education, the program also aims to provide a comprehensive package of services—nutrition, health and social services. The idea is to give disadvantaged 3 and 4-year-olds a "head start" in kindergarten by providing a rich preschool experience. And so Head Start is modeled after preschools and, like typical private nursery schools, meets only during the school year and only in half-day sessions.

"The positive benefits of Head Start are targeted toward the educational needs of the child and are not meant to help provide child care for low-income women," Berheide said.

Several proposals now circulating on Capitol Hill would allow Head Start to provide full-day, full-year sessions and also to take in toddlers. But to do so wouldn't be cheap: One proposed plan would cost $13 billion when fully implemented after five years.

A crazy quilt of programs addresses the mother's needs, but with little attention to the children's. The 1988 Family Support Act provided child care support to welfare parents in school or job training programs and, once they got a job, for a year's transition into the economic mainstream. Two 1990 laws, the Child Care and Development Block Grant Act and the At-Risk Child Care Act, together provide about $1 billion a year to subsidize child care for poor families whether they're on welfare or not.

The subsidies "are seen like transportation—a supportive service to get the mother to work, rather than a co-equal service in order to make sure that the child succeeds in this world," said Judith M. Rosen, who directs the Fairfax County (Va.) Office for Children.

Consequently, the government's priority is keeping down costs. Welfare regulations pay mothers only up to 75 per cent of the local median cost for child care. The regulations for child care block grants, while somewhat less severe, don't emphasize quality.

"We give parents this impossible dilemma of deciding between putting their child in a part-time day program [Head Start] and then patching together something in the afternoon in order to get full-time employment, or going the route of the Family Support Act and potentially subjecting their children to poor quality care," child care expert Phillips said.

And that's only the beginning of the problem. The plethora of subsidy programs amounts to an obstacle course for beneficiaries. In 1988, the General Accounting Office (GAO) counted 46 federal programs for specific aspects of child care—subsidizing milk for children in some day care centers, for example, or providing child care at military installations.

Marcia K. Meyers, a researcher at the University of California (Berkeley), studied the impact of child care subsidies on participants in California's education and training program for welfare recipients.

The red tape, she found, was cumbersome and utterly confusing, "Only a small fraction [of people] hung on to the child care subsidies," she said in an interview. "Sometimes they'd never heard of the program. Or somebody had told them, 'Don't bother, the waiting lists are too long.' Or it was just too much trouble on top of everything else to get themselves down to yet another welfare office to apply for benefits."

The bottom line, Meyers concluded, was that those who had difficulty obtaining child care and those who were concerned about the quality of the care they did get or worried about the safety of their children were much likelier to drop out of the program and go back on welfare.

In Fairfax County, Rosen has managed to untangle the federal bureaucratic knots and to weave the various subsidies into a seamless program. "It's nearly impossible for us logistically," she said, "but we can do it because we have the authority over all those funding streams."

Getting welfare mothers into the work force is the central theme of Clinton's welfare reform plan. But child care experts warn this won't happen unless his plan helps to provide quality child care. They also urge that barriers between the different child care subsidies be removed and that Head Start be linked to other low-income child care programs.

"Flawed as they may be, these [federal] programs uncapped the demand," CDF's Blank said. "Families realized, 'Hey, there's a program out there that can help me,' So we're back with waiting lists that are as long as, if not longer than, when we started."

Low-income families spend up to 25 per cent of their incomes on child care, according to the Census Bureau. A 1991 study by the GAO looked at the potential for poor single mothers to work themselves above the poverty line. The GAO figured that 65 per cent could do so if they could find full-time, year-round jobs and didn't have to pay for day care. But if they had to pay for child care, the proportion slipped to only 45 per cent.

No matter how anyone slices it, however, there isn't enough subsidy money to go around. Welfare is an entitlement: Anyone who's eligible can participate. But the states have to come up with matching funds to get federal child care subsidies, and many have been too fiscally strapped to do so. Meanwhile, the Head Start and child care block grant programs can distribute only as much money as Congress makes available each year. So, in Fairfax County, for example, while the number of subsidized child care slots has soared 70 per cent in the past three years, the waiting lists are also longer than ever before.

Headaches and Hassles

For the poor, money is probably the biggest child care headache. For the middle class, availability may be a bigger problem than affordability.

Middle-class families, in fact, get the lion's share of federal child care subsidies. Sandra L. Hofferth, who researches child care issues at the Urban Institute, calculated that 60 per cent of the $7 billion in federal child care subsidies in 1991 went out through the Child and Dependent Care Tax Credit.

Although the working poor can apply for the tax credit, Hofferth found that only 22 per cent of families with annual incomes of less than $15,000 do so (compared with 37 per cent of families with annual incomes of more than $50,000). Because the credit is nonrefundable, only families that earn enough to pay taxes can use it. And the because the care giver's social security number must be reported on federal tax forms, those who deal in the day care underground can't take advantage of the credit, either.

There is considerable political support for increasing and broadening this form of child care subsidy by making the tax credit refundable; raising the earned-income tax credit for working-poor families with children and perhaps issuing child care vouchers that could be used anywhere on the open market.

"If you put more money in the pockets of working parents, obviously there's more money available to pay child care providers and to pay for higher-quality child care," said Elaine Ciulla Kamarck, a senior fellow at the Progressive Policy Institute, a Washington think tank that has the President's ear on a range of economic issues. "Rich people don't have a child care crisis. Markets do, at some level, work."

Indeed, at his televised town meeting in Southfield, Mich., on Feb. 10, Clinton responded to a question about child care with a plug for expanding the tax credits. He also called for a federal-state partnership to improve the quality of child care nationwide.

Most child care experts agree that tax credits or vouchers, however, won't solve the problem. There's no evidence that families who save money by claiming the tax credit, for example, use it to buy higher-quality child care.

"We've got to do both [subsidize parents and support quality programs] because [a high-quality child care] system just doesn't exist," said Barbara A. Willer, the public affairs director of the Washington-based National Association for the Education of Young Children. "We need to ensure that families have a range of child care options. But those choices are false choices unless there are strong systems and programs. So we need to target money in sufficient quantity to operate good programs."

The child care problem isn't a lack of providers. "We've pretty much shown that there are sufficient places out there—you can find child care," Hofferth said, referring to the 1990 survey that she conducted with Willer and others. "The key issue is, is it good?"

Rich or poor, families in need of child care say that the first, and sometimes the steepest, hurdle is finding out what kind of care is available in their communities.

In the business, this is called resource and referral. Although most states and communities have a resource and referral system, information about child care options doesn't reach most of the parents who need it.

Peg Smith, the deputy director of Indiana's bureau of child develop, said that one of the first things she discovered on the job is a pervasive information gap—a gap that the state aims to fill through a comprehensive planning effort. "The state of Indiana invests a great deal of money into resource and referral," she said, "So we have to face the fact that something still isn't working. We may have to change some things."

Once parents find a day care provider, how can they judge quality? One way is to ascertain whether the provider is trained and whether the facility is licensed, Indiana's planning effort, for example, is also looking into upgrading licensing procedures for day care centers and training programs for providers.

Indiana's program is partially financed by the 1990 child care block grant program, which directed states to set aside a small portion of their funds for such quality improvements. Although similar activities are under way in other states, the Indiana initiative is considered more comprehensive than most. But even enthusiasts admit that these campaigns have a very long way to go.

Regulating day care is a state and local responsibility. But when the GAO surveyed stated regulations and enforcement last year, it came up with a dismal picture. All states require commercial and work-based day care facilities to be licensed, but 32 states exempt at least some school-based centers and 12 exempt church-

based centers. Although 28 states say that they license at least
some home-based day care centers, as many as 92 per cent are
actually unregulated. Monitoring and enforcement of standards
at regulated facilities in many states is minimal, the GAO found.

"So they have these standards, but are they able to enforce
them in a complete way?" said Janet L. Mascia, an author of the
GAO study. "If you think of all the providers in a state as a pie, the
states are really only looking at a very small slice of that pie."

As part of a larger child care study, Phillips and several colleagues visited day care centers in Georgia, Massachusetts and
Virginia to check on whether they complied with state-mandated
ratios of staff to children. The ratios are strictest for infants and,
not surprisingly, compliance was worst in this category. In Georgia, which has the most lenient ratio, 72 per cent of the centers
were in compliance. In Massachusetts, which has the most-
stringent standards, only 55 per cent of the centers were in compliance. Virginia was in the middle, at 63 per cent.

On the other hand, local ordinances and other regulations
can sometimes be so intrusive and unnecessary as to drive providers out of the business or into the underground. "Our child
care system is characterized by both regulatory neglect and regulatory overkill," said William Gormley, a public policy professor at
Georgetown University who studies child care regulations. "It's a
curious combination of overly strict and overly lenient regulations."

In Milwaukee County, Wis., a middle-class suburban area,
Gormley figured that family day care providers had to make an
average of $936 in home improvements to pass the licensing
requirements—replacing kitchen fixtures and bathtubs and adding an exit door, for example. Dekalb County, Ga., requires them
to run "a gantlet of inspections, including building, electrical and
plumbing inspections," Gormley said. "Eight out of 10 providers
simply ignore these requirements."

While the experts agree that reasonable standards are vital
and credible enforcement is crucial, they say that regulations are
sometimes misdirected.

"It's not like inspecting meat," Phillips said. "The best form of
regulation accomplishes two things: It provides education and
support and it reduces the isolation of child care providers."

Indiana, for example, commissioned a series of training videos for day care providers that were broadcast on cable television
during the children's nap time.

The quality question pretty much boils down to money: how much the providers of child care are paid. Whitebook's surveys show that college graduates in the child care field earn $11,000–$12,000 a year. To make $20,000 or more a year, a child care provider has to get out of the playroom and run a school.

Borrowing an idea from Head Start, where salaries are higher, the California welfare-to-jobs program looked at a scheme to train welfare mothers to become child care workers. "Then they realized the women couldn't make enough money doing [child care] to get off welfare," Whitebook said.

Laurie Meltzer Klinovsky [is] a teacher who directs the Greenwood School in Hyattsville, Md., a private preschool that provides day care for the Centers for Disease Control and Prevention and several other federal agencies that have offices in the same complex. "If you you're doing it to make money, you might as well get out of the business right now," Klinovsky said. "I do it because I like to do what I'm doing."

"We've really only put our toe in the water on the child care issue," CDF's Blank said. "Eventually, we're going to have to figure out how to finance this. And it can't be on the back of the child care workers. It won't happen without some funding mechanism. And it's going to be complicated."

MARY POPPINS SPEAKS OUT[3]

Nannies: dark-skinned women from Trinidad and El Salvador, watching tow-haired charges play in the sand. Fresh-faced Americans from the heartland, eager for adventure—if only their employers would come home before 10 p.m. and relieve them. Medical students from Poland, farm girls from Ireland, teachers from Grenada, many struggling to send money home to their own kids while minding someone else's amid a sea of American toys. Their voices haven't been heard much in the debate over attorney general or the hardships of American working mothers. Even feminists have largely ignored them, forgetting that as wom-

[3]Article by Melinda Beck. From *Newsweek* 121(8):66–68 F 22 '93. Copyright © 1993 by Newsweek, Inc. Reprinted with permission.

en have moved into traditionally male jobs, they've had to find other women to take their place in the home. "Those women tend to be poor, working-class and usually of color," says sociologist Mary Romero, author of "Maid in the U.S.A." "It reminds me of Sojourner Truth's statement: 'Ain't *I* a woman?'"

Zoë Baird and Kimba Wood weren't the only victims of Nannygate. Placement agencies are getting calls from families suddenly desperate to find *legal* sitters. "People are panicking," says Eileen Stein of the Gilbert Child Care Agency in Manhattan. Trusted cleaning ladies are being asked embarrassing questions about their taxes and shadow income. High-school babysitters' clubs are jittery too, fearing that families will stop going out to dinner rather than run afoul of the $50-per-quarter social-security rule. Meanwhile, some documented workers are flaunting their status. Spotted on a Manhattan street last week: a nanny pushing a stroller with a blowup of her green card attached to the front.

It's a measure of how haphazard child care is in America that nobody can say how many such workers there are—or even agree on what to call them. The International Nanny Association in Austin, Texas, says there are 75,000 to 100,000 "professional, experienced nannies" in the United States. The Bureau of Labor Statistics counted 353,000 full- and part-time "in-home child care" workers last year. That number mysteriously dropped during the 1980s, at a time when mothers with young children went to work in record numbers. But with the vast majority of even legal sitters paid off the books, it's not surprising that some aren't eager to answer government questionnaires. The number of illegal workers is anybody's guess. But, says Lisa Schanzer of Family Extensions Inc., a Connecticut placement agency: "If you sent every illegal in this country home, you'd have a disaster overnight."

Among nannies themselves, reaction to Nannygate is as diverse as their ethnic backgrounds and range of duties. To Zawanda Washington, a 31-year-old American nanny in Dallas, the whole incident shed new light on how cheap many parents are when it comes to child care: "People don't want to pay what it takes to hire someone qualified." Washington can't complain herself—she earns more than $400 a week caring for two children, 4 and 7; she has her own room and bath, paid sick leave, paid health insurance and time to take piano lessons. She also has a master's degree in sociology and two years' training at a prestigious British nanny school. "People with my education and experience expect, bottom line, at least $350 a week," she says.

Graduates of American "nanny academies," which blossomed in the 1980s, have similar feelings. Along with CPR, child psychology and bathing techniques, most schools hammer home the gospel of "professionalism" and the need to be paid on the books. "If somebody wanted to hire you to work in an office and said they wouldn't pay social security, you'd get up and leave," says Joy Shelton, who heads the American Council of Nanny Schools. But "trained" U.S. nannies say the abundance of illegal workers in some areas pulls wages down for everyone—and devalues the field. "I think families are risking the welfare of their children when they hire illegals," says Jennifer Healy, 20, who graduated from a Colorado nanny school last year and now cares for 7-month-old Sarah in New York. "In most cases, illegals don't have the training that I got. What if there is an emergency? Would they know what to do?"

Tell that to an immigrant nanny, however, and get set for an earful. "I don't think you have to go to school to learn what to do," says "Stephanie," a native of Jamaica who is now a U.S. citizen. She, too, is fighting for more respect for her field. "People tell me that I could get a better job." But she loves caring for the 3-year-old daughter of two journalists. "Americans say, West Indians come and take our jobs. But would they do this work? A lot of Americans aren't into baby-sitting. They'd rather go to the office."

Many illegals have advanced degrees from their home countries—and the gumption to seek better opportunities. The America they find rarely matches the milk-and-honey stories they heard. The cost of living is higher, the work conditions are harder, and the wait to obtain legal status has stretched longer and longer. "Anita" breaks into tears when she tells of leaving her children, then 3, 6 and 9, behind in the Philippines in 1986. "As a mother, it was hard, but I have dreams for them," she says. One of those dreams is to have them join her in America—and when her employers started the legalization process, she was told it would take three years. That was fours years ago. "Yesterday the lawyer told me she can't say how much longer it will be. It's moving slower and slower." In the meantime, Anita sends $350 home each month; $1,000 buys a full year of tuition for her children. But she has nightmares that she will never see them again. The Zoë Baird incident has left her even more fearful: "I'm afraid

they will send us home," she sobs, "and I won't have enough
savings to send my children to college."

So scared. Behind every illegal is a story of enterprise and
sacrifice. "Flor" came the hard way from Peru in 1986 when she
was 20. Her family scraped to buy what they thought was safe
transit for her, but she was abandoned in Panama, robbed, and
had to work her way overland through Honduras, Guatemala and
Mexico. She made a midnight sprint across the border at Tijuana.
"Everyone running with me was caught. A policeman with a gun
told me to stop, but I didn't. I was so scared." She hid under a car,
was smuggled through safe houses by paid coyotes, often packed
in tiny quarters with dozens of others. Finally, she joined her
brother in New York City and a family gave her a chance as a
part-time nanny for their 4-week-old daughter, even though Flor
spoke no English. "They had faith that I would learn," she says.
The family also helped sponsor her; she won her legal papers last
summer. She now has a husband, a 2-year-old son, and plans to
attend college next fall. "Someday I will tell my son my story, so he
can do better," she says. She has no complaints about Zoë Baird:
"She was giving an opportunity to somebody."

All too often, nannies aren't treated so well—and illegals are
particularly vulnerable to exploitation. They feel powerless to
complain in the face of outrageous demands—even sexual advances from employers. But a few are fighting back. "Roselia," an
illegal from El Salvador, worked for one year for a Los Angeles
family that made her sleep on the kitchen floor, piled chores on
her, then fired her, still owing her much of the $100-a-week they
had agreed to pay. Emboldened after she won a work permit for
another job, Roselia sued them for back pay last year, and won a
$5,000 default judgment when they failed to show up in court.

Fighting back. Like employers, most illegals were surprised to
learn that even undocumented workers are expected to file social-
security taxes. Many are still reluctant to leave a paper trail or
take deductions from their earnings. But more and more domestic workers are hearing that amassing Worker Compensation, unemployment insurance and retirement benefits is well worth the
hit in cash flow. Donna Brazile, chief of staff to Rep. Eleanor
Holmes Norton, spreads that message tirelessly. Brazile's mother
worked as a domestic for 22 years in New Orleans, caring for a
white family's three children, and later *their* children, as well as
raising her own nine kids. Brazile says she didn't mind that other
kids saw more of her mother than she did. The real indignity

came when her mother suffered heart problems and applied for disability benefits, in 1988, only to find there was no record of her with the Social Security Administration. She died a few months later at 52. "My mother bought into the cash system. And I understand it—believe me," says Brazile. "But I'm telling low-income black women to get into the system. In the long haul, it's worth it. The last thing a domestic worker needs at the end of a hard life is not to have benefits."

Whatever their legal or tax status, most nannies agree on one thing: Americans should value their kids more. Some families do stretch their budgets to provide good care, and treat their employees fairly. But as nannies know better than anyone, others spend more money and time on their cars, and their VCRs, than on the people who care for their children. INA president Kelly Campbell, herself a nanny, says: "Until we get to the point where we value our children as much as our material possessions, we're going to have problems with child care." And problems, too, with the people who provide it.

NANNYGATE FOR THE POOR[4]

For years, Gladys Cordero was pointed out by strangers as "the lady in the green house." She cared for as many as 16 children at once in her modest home on Staten Island—illegally. Neighbors knew her. Cabdrivers directed customers to her. Even the public elementary school across the street sent parents her way.

A loyal clientele trailed the 60-year-old woman three years ago, when she moved to a new neighborhood 40 blocks away. Mrs. Cordero charges $20 a day for babies in diapers and $15 for older children. But the real currency is trust, she said, in a widespread commerce that has served struggling, low-income parents for decades in New York City.

Officials say there is no way of knowing how many people like Mrs. Cordero provide illegal day care. She cares for three preschoolers and an 11-month-old grandson in her home in South

[4]Article by Lynda Richardson. From *The New York Times* My 2 '93:53. Copyright © 1993 by the New York Times Company. Reprinted with permission.

Beach, S.I. But with more women working and more mothers providing the sole support for their family, child-care advocates suggest there could be at least 25,000 day-care providers operating without licenses or official oversight in the city's working poor neighborhoods.

One city official called the largely invisible world of these day care operations the "poor person's nannygate"—the flip side of the highly publicized troubles of Zoë Baird and Kimba Wood, President Clinton's first two choices for Attorney General. Both were forced to withdraw their names after questions were raised about their hiring of illegal aliens as nannies.

Nowhere Else to Turn

Nationwide, there are from 550,000 to 1.1 million unlicensed family day-care homes, according to a 1991 study commissioned by the Federal Government. The study also showed that households with incomes under $15,000 spend an average of 23 percent on child care, while families with incomes over $40,000 spend an average of 6 percent.

In New York City, day care subsidized by the city serves only 13 percent of the parents who are eligible. A vast majority are left to find day care on their own. Many low-income parents who typically can afford to pay only $50 to $75 a week, ultimately turn to neighbors or relatives or even strangers whose names are posted on telephone poles or community bulletin boards.

City officials fear that such arrangements might expose children to unnecessary hazards. Providers might be caring for a dangerously high number of children, not meeting fire and safety codes or, in rare cases, might have a history of abuse or neglect.

In February [1993], two children died in a house fire in Queens at an unregistered day-care operation run by an 82-year-old woman. But officials stressed that the Queens fire was unusual, the first such fire since two children entrusted to an illegal day-care provider in Brooklyn died seven years ago.

'Not Day-Care Cops'

For every child under the age of 3 in regulated care in New York City, 15 children of that age are entrusted to illegal providers, estimates Child Care Inc., the largest nonprofit resource and day-care referral agency in the city.

"People are desperate for care, and they want to believe their baby sitters are adequate to the job because it's hard to face the possibility that it might not be true," said Caroline Zinsser, an expert on informal and unregulated day care in New York. "Unlicensed care is not necessarily bad, but when you get into dealing with strangers, a license is a help in assuring quality."

State law requires certification for any person who cares for more than two children not related to the provider. The day-care providers must pass physical exams, be checked for child abuse and neglect and subject their places of business to random inspections. The requirements become more stringent the more children a provider cares for.

The city's Department of Health is responsible for the inspections and enforcement. But city officials, as well as child-care advocates, concede there is not an aggressive effort to root out illegal operations because of inadequate staffing and recent budget cuts.

"We're in the business of facilitating day care," said Steven Matthews, a spokesman for the city's Department of Health. "We're not day-care cops. If we become aware of a center, we will move to bring it into compliance."

Among the reasons that many providers do not comply with regulations are a desire to avoid taxes, a disdain for government intrusion and a fear that they may lose welfare benefits because of the income. Some are intimidated by the red tape, while others, like Mrs. Cordero, simply see no need for it. "I never thought of it," she said. "The time flies."

Yolanda Cutler, a single mother in Jamaica, Queens, saw the merits of having a licensed provider. But when she could not find one for less than $100 a week for her 3-year-old daughter, she took a chance on a stranger whose phone number was tacked to a supermarket bulletin board for $75 a week.

The provider cares for four young children as well as five of her own in a tiny apartment in Queens. In the last six months, Ms. Cutler said she has been unhappy that her daughter, Mischalett, is allowed to watch television all day. She is unnerved by the cats that race about the provider's home, the litter box by the front door and the perilously steep stairway.

But the 21-year-old Ms. Cutler, who studies social work at York College by day and rings a cash register at a Burger King at night, says her options are limited. She earns $6,000 a year and lives with her mother.

"It's not up to my standards, but right now it's the best thing I could do," Ms. Cutler said.

On the Waiting List

Vivian Jones, a single mother, feels the same way. Every day, her two children, still in diapers, are dropped off at the apartment of an illegal day-care provider, known as "Auntie" by neighbors along Amsterdam Avenue in Washington Heights.

Ms. Jones, a secretary who makes less than $20,000 a year, worries about the arrangement. But she said she received little help from the government when she sought day care.

In January [1993], Ms. Jones applied for day care that would have cost her only $35 a week with the Agency for Child Development, the city agency that administers subsidized day care. But the 25-year-old mother said she was told that there was nothing available on the West Side of Manhattan for children the age of hers, 10-month-old Shafonda and 22-month-old Rondell. Ms. Jones's name was added to a waiting list.

Ms. Jones said she could not afford to wait. She recently found an illegal day-care provider through a network of relatives and friends. She pays $100 a week for her children to spend 10 hours a day with the provider.

"She's a known person," Ms. Jones said. "She has raised a lot of children in the neighborhood for over 12 years."

The day-care provider, like many others, declined to be interviewed. Ms. Jones said her children's provider, who cares for three babies and two school-age children, chooses not to become regulated because, she says, "It's too much hassle."

On her first visit, she was heartened that the provider was open and friendly. There was a smoke detector. The provider's fifth-floor apartment in a tenement building was spacious, clean and free of graffiti. "It doesn't even stink when you go in," Ms. Jones said.

Ms. Jones, who considered quitting her job to care for her children, would have been given a higher priority for subsidized care if she had been on welfare, an abuse and neglect victim or a teen-age parent, said city officials and child-care advocates. But she describes herself as an independent woman and is loath to join the welfare rolls.

"I'm focusing on working instead of depending on the system," she said in frustration. "It's hard for somebody who's motivated to work to find proper care for their children."

Ms. Jones said she would have preferred to have her children in regulated day care, but she made her decision out of necessity.

"I can't take my kids to work and I don't want to quit my job," she said. "You have to use what you can use and keep going. You are always going to worry because you don't really know what people are going to do behind closed doors. You ask God to bless the children and protect them and watch over them."

Licensing Process Changed

Last year, the state changed its licensing process to encourage illegal day-care providers to comply with regulations. Providers no longer must be inspected by officials before getting a license; they must simply fill out a long application form to become automatically certified.

But advocates say the daunting, English-only form and a fear of an Internal Revenue Service crackdown has only discouraged potential providers and driven even more underground.

City officials concede there have been problems. But Mr. Matthews, of the health department, said the application forms have been shortened. If the process were simplified more, he said, "you would run the risk of 'What value is the regulation?'"

"The whole idea," he said, "is to have certain requirements and standards."

The penalty for operating without registering can run as high as $500 a day and the closing of the illegal sites. Since the February fire in Queens, city officials said they received a flurry of calls from parents inquiring whether their day care was legal. But in the last eight months, no fines have been levied for operating without proper registration, said James McCormack, a deputy director at the city's Department of Health.

Patricia Lee, who provides day care for three children on Coney Island, said the fire in the home in Queens had only a fleeting impact on the parents who live in the high-rise projects in her neighborhood.

"That was something tragic," she said. "But when people are looking for a baby sitter, they don't mention the Queens apartment. They're not that meticulous about apartments or smoke alarms. They want to know if they feel comfortable knowing you won't hurt their children. We don't have too much choice out here."

ENFORCING CHILD-CARE STANDARDS[5]

In light of new federal initiatives to fund child care for families in need, many states are considering the question of whether
standards for child care providers ought to be reduced to promote parental choice, increased to ensure the safety and well-
being of children, or altered to accommodate both goals. As
policymakers begin to grapple with this question, they must also
consider the question of enforcement. The fact that standards are
on the books does not, of course, automatically result in compliance by providers. Only through enforcement of those standards
can any level of government, or parents who place their children
in the care of others, be assured that minimum requirements are
met.

The federal government, having funded child care primarily
through the Social Services Block Grant for some years, has now
expanded its interest in this area through the Family Support Act
of 1988 (FSA) and the Omnibus Budget Reconciliation Act of
1990 (OBRA 90). Under FSA, states are required to provide child
care for participants in the Job Opportunities and Basic Skills
Training Program, for Aid to Families with Dependent Children
(AFDC) recipients who need such care in order to work, and for
former AFDC recipients for up to 12 months after becoming
ineligible for AFDC as a result of increased earnings. OBRA
90 created the Child Care and Development Block Grant
(CC&DBG) and the Title IV-A At-Risk Child Care program.
CC&DBG funds are directed toward providing child care and
related services for low-income families and improving access to
quality child care for all families, while At-Risk Child Care funds
are intended to provide child care for low-income families who
are at risk of becoming dependent on AFDC.

With these programs have come legislative and regulatory
directives to states concerning the standards they may set for
providers receiving federal funds. Under proposed regulations
issued by the U.S. Department of Health and Human Services
(HHS) for implementing the At-Risk Child Care program, states

[5]Article by Penny R. Thompson and Nancy J. Molyneaux. From *Public Welfare*
50(1):20–25 Winter 1992. Reprinted with permission.

would be limited in their use of a two-tiered system of standard setting that differentiates between publicly and privately funded child care. Such a system sets one standard—presumably more stringent—for care paid for with public funds, and another standard—presumably more relaxed—for care paid for with private funds. Under the proposed rules, while states can still set different standards for care depending on the source of payment, they cannot refuse to pay for care funded under Title IV-A of the Social Security Act simply because such care did not meet the higher standard set for publicly funded care.

This policy contrasts with that of the CC&DBG, in which legislative language is clear that states may set more stringent standards for providers receiving block grant money than those for other providers. In addition, the providers receiving funds under the block grant must meet certain minimal standards for prevention and control of infectious diseases, building safety, and health and safety training. In some states, this might mean that providers traditionally exempt from state regulation—small group child care or care by sectarian organizations, for example—now might have to face a more stringent set of requirements in order to provide services reimbursable with block grant money, although according to federal regulations implementing this legislation, such standards may not have the effect of limiting availability of child care services.

Observing how states respond to these directives will be interesting. For the sake of simplicity, some states may decide to raise their standards across the board, requiring all child care to meet a new and more stringent set of requirements, regardless of source of payment or setting. Others may drop standards so as not to affect access to care. Regardless of the direction states take, federal policies concerning standard setting clearly have touched a nerve in states and localities that traditionally have considered the question of standards theirs and theirs alone.

Yet, for all the current posturing over the issue of the federal role in setting standards—and certainly more is to come as the implications of new programs and rules become clearer—we must not make too much of standards. By themselves, standards can be meaningless, no matter how stringent they are or to whom they apply. Without effective monitoring and enforcement, standards assure very little.

Historically, the federal government has taken a laissez-faire attitude towards the states' enforcement of standards. Despite the problem by wearing baggy clothes and avoiding other people.

This demoralizing, debilitating, and sometimes deadly condition is anorexia nervosa. Although the Greek and Latin roots of the words mean "lack of appetite of nervous origin," that description is not quite accurate. Appetite—which is often normal, at least at first—is not even mentioned in the standard psychiatric definition. Researchers are still trying to learn why these women want to starve themselves and how to prevent them from succeeding.

A person with anorexia is likely to be depressed, anxious, irritable, and insomniac. Her joints may become swollen, her hair and skin dry, her nails brittle. She is often lethargic and constipated. She loses bone mass (sometimes permanently), and if she is young enough, her sexual development may be arrested. Most important, her body temperature, heart rate, and blood pressure can fall to dangerously low levels. Loss of potassium may cause heart arrhythmias. Death from cardiac arrest can occur, as can suicide.

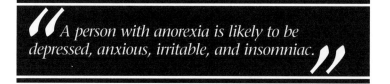

A person with anorexia is likely to be depressed, anxious, irritable, and insomniac.

About one in 200 persons in the United States will develop anorexia nervosa at some time. Ninety percent are women. On average, the diagnosis is first made at age 18, but symptoms may arise in much older and much younger people. People with anorexia have a high rate of bulimia, the bingeing and purging syndrome. They are also susceptible to major depression (a rate of 50%–75%) and obsessive-compulsive disorder (a 25% rate).

Symptoms of Anorexia Nervosa

A person has anorexia nervosa when:

• She (or, occasionally, he) refuses to maintain weight at a normal level. Her weight is 15% below the healthy minimum.

• She shows intense fear of gaining weight or becoming fat.

• She has disturbed ideas about her weight or body shape, tends to judge her value as a person by her weight or body shape, or denies that her weight loss is a serious problem.

• If she is a woman of the appropriate age, she has not

menstruated for at least three consecutive cycles.

Anorexia nervosa takes two forms:

• Restricting (dieting, fasting, and compulsive exercise)

• Binge eating/purging (deliberate vomiting or misuse of laxatives, enemas, or diuretics in addition to dieting, fasting, and exercise).

The Genetic Background

Eating disorders run in families. In one recent study, the risk for anorexia in relatives of a person with the disorder turned out to be 11 times higher than average. Studies comparing identical with fraternal twins indicate that the heritability of anorexia (the proportion of individual variability associated with genetic difference) is about 55%.

These statistics have inspired a search for susceptibility genes. Last year [2002], European researchers announced that 11% of anorexics, compared to 4.5% of controls, carried a certain form of the gene for a hormone that stimulates appetite. According to a 2002 report, some people with the restricting type of anorexia nervosa (those who don't binge and purge) have an unusual variant of a gene that affects the reabsorption of the neurotransmitter norepinephrine.

> *About one in 200 persons in the United States will develop anorexia nervosa at some time.*

A strain of hogs bred for low fat may provide further data on anorexia susceptibility genes. Some of the hogs are highly active, eat little, and waste away. Researchers are trying to learn whether any similar genetic patterns occur in people suffering from anorexia.

Psychology of Self-Starvation

Physicians have been speculating inconclusively about the psychological roots of anorexia for hundreds of years. Especially in the 20th century, they've suggested a wide range of possible influences, from peer pressure to sexual anxieties and child abuse.

According to one theory, anorexia is a kind of addiction.

The German word for the disorder, Pubert tsmagersucht, means "craving for thinness at puberty." One striking characteristic drug addicts and anorexics often have in common is denial—unwillingness to admit that they have a problem. But most experts find more dissimilarities than similarities between anorexia and substance abuse.

There may be something like an anorexic personality, however. Girls and women with the disorder are often shy, neat, quiet, conscientious, and hypersensitive to rejection. They are prey to irrational guilt, feelings of inferiority, and obsessive worrying. They have unrealistic hopes of perfection and feel as though they can never meet their own standards.

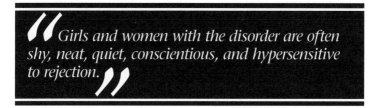

Girls and women with the disorder are often shy, neat, quiet, conscientious, and hypersensitive to rejection.

Anorexia could be a way some young women with this kind of personality respond to the demands of adulthood. They don't want to be average or admit weakness, but they fear asserting themselves. Their sexual desires and the prospect of independence from their families frighten them. Instead of acknowledging their fears, they try to restore order to their lives by manipulating their weight with compulsive fasting and physical activity.

In that way they exercise some control over their lives. By denying their own physical needs, they show that they won't allow others to dictate them. Falling numbers on the scale are an achievement—a victory over themselves and others. At the same time, by starving themselves and preventing menstruation, they convey the message they don't want to grow up yet.

Some clinicians who treat anorexia believe that, in adolescents at least, the blame lies with parents who make conflicting demands. The theory is that the parents, in effect, tell their daughter to show a capacity for adult independence without separating herself from the family. In the family systems theory of anorexia, it's seen as a defense that maintains the family's otherwise precarious stability. A daughter who refuses to eat may be trying to hold a disintegrating family together by providing a common object of concern for her parents. Or, just the opposite—the family may be "enmeshed," meaning that its boundaries and responsibilities are not distinct. Its members are overprotective of one another; they don't acknowledge feelings or resolve conflicts. According to this theory, anorexia may arise if the family's rules and roles are too inflexible to change as a daughter grows up.

Fasting and Culture

It's sometimes said that eating disorders in general and anorexia nervosa in particular are largely products of modern Western upper-class and middle-class society. "You can't be too rich or too thin," as the Duchess of Windsor is supposed to have said. In industrial countries, the average woman is becoming heavier, while the body regarded as ideal for health and beauty becomes slimmer. Being happy and successful, women are told, goes with being thin. As a result, more than half of American women, including many young girls, say they are on a diet.

Of course, the vast majority of people who diet don't have an eating disorder. But the more intense this kind of social pressure is, the more likely it seems that a troubled young woman will develop anorexia rather than (or in addition to) other psychiatric symptoms. And now, the argument goes, anorexia, along with bulimia and obesity, is beginning to infect the non-Western world, carried by television, films, and advertisements.

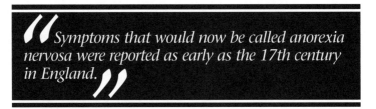

Symptoms that would now be called anorexia nervosa were reported as early as the 17th century in England.

But research has shown that it's not so simple. Symptoms that would now be called anorexia nervosa were reported as early as the 17th century in England. Descriptions of similar symptoms also appear in ancient Chinese and Persian manuscripts and in African tribal lore. Today, many studies show no clear relationship between severe eating disorders and social class or the influence of Western culture.

There is some (disputed) evidence that women in non-Western countries are, on the average, less dissatisfied with their bodies, but that doesn't necessarily imply a lower probability of anorexia. In the United States, whites report more mild eating disturbances than African Americans, but the two groups have about the same rate of clinical eating disorders, including anorexia. Although middle-class anorexia patients may get more attention, it has not been shown that anorexia is a function of social class, either.

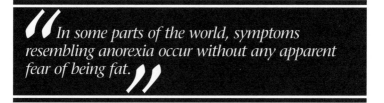

In some parts of the world, symptoms resembling anorexia occur without any apparent fear of being fat.

Women with anorexia may not even be especially prone to over-estimating the size of their bodies. One study comparing anorexic with healthy women of the same height and weight found that both groups overestimated their size by about the same amount. The anorexic women were more anxious about their body shape only because they had unreasonable standards.

Fasting and Religion

In some parts of the world, symptoms resembling anorexia occur without any apparent fear of being fat. Anorexic women in Hong Kong may say that they have family problems, their appetite is poor, or they simply don't know why they can't eat. In Ghana, women with anorexic symptoms often say they are fasting for religious reasons.

In medieval Europe, for some centuries, fasting almost unto death was regarded as a sign of holiness—a withdrawal from the world and the flesh. One famous medieval ascetic was St. Catherine of Siena, who died at age 32 in 1379, apparently from the effects of starvation. She wrote, "Make a supreme effort to root out that self-love from your heart and to plant in its place this holy self-hatred. This is the royal road by which we turn our back on mediocrity and which leads us without fail to the summit of perfection."

Today's anorexic girls and young women often confess similar thoughts of self-denial and self-perfection. The American Psychiatric Association now classifies a condition with all the symptoms of anorexia nervosa except an obsession with body shape or size as an example of an "eating disorder not otherwise specified."

It's possible that cultures supply only the justification for self-starvation rather than its cause. Some feminists have proposed that women who refuse to eat are misguided rebels making an inarticulate social protest. By refusing to develop a woman's body, they are rejecting a woman's place, whatever that may be in a given culture. Their refusal to eat is a way to show that they are exceptional. How they describe what they are doing—dieting to become thin or fasting to become holy, for example—may depend on the social pressures and opportunities they face.

2

The Signs of Anorexia

Roberto Eguia and Alicia Bello

Roberto Eguia and Alicia Bello are members of the Argentine Asociacion de Lucha Contra Bulimia y Anorexia (the Argentine Association to Fight Bulimia and Anorexia).

Anorexia is appearing with increasing frequency among adolescents of both sexes. Effective treatment often depends on early detection of anorexia symptoms. This is usually difficult, however, because anorexia sufferers try to hide the behaviors typically associated with their disorder. Because of the amount of time they spend with young people, parents and teachers are in the best position to detect the beginning symptoms of anorexia, which often include skipping meals and snacks at school and at home, excessive physical exercise, perfectionism, personality changes, feelings of shame about their bodies, and self-induced vomiting.

Thirty years ago, there was no record of anorexia nervosa and bulimia anywhere in the world. Not because physicians and psychiatrists lacked the tools to detect these disorders, but because the boom of waif-like thinness had not yet invaded western women's collective imagination.

Until the 1960s when Twiggy's skeletal figure traipsed down the catwalk, fashion's spotlight illuminated voluptuous bodies, with the odd little bulge tucked away here and there. Today, however, eating disorders are appearing with an alarming and increasing frequency among adolescents who are obsessed with achieving the "physical ideal." Anorexia and bulimia are appearing at increasingly younger ages and among both sexes (young men currently account for 10% of those suffering from eating disorders).

Thinness is associated with success, power, beauty and status. No wonder "miracle" diets seem a sure way to triumph. These obsessions can lead to serious illness, such as anorexia nervosa, characterized by exaggerated weight loss, or bulimia, in which episodes of bingeing (ingesting large amounts of food) alternate with "compensatory" behavior (such as self-induced vomiting, abuse of laxatives, diuretics, anorexic agents or excessive physical activity).

According to the World Health Organization the mortality rate among those diagnosed with anorexia is 15%.

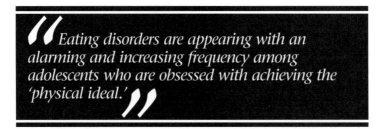

Eating disorders are appearing with an alarming and increasing frequency among adolescents who are obsessed with achieving the 'physical ideal.'

Argentina's ALUBA (Asociacion de Lucha contra Bulimia y Anorexia, Association to Fight Bulimia and Anorexia) is a nongovernmental organization founded and directed by Dr. Mabel Belle. For the past fifteen years, ALUBA has been recognized as a pioneer and leader in the field of eating disorders in Argentina and abroad. Since its creation, ALUBA has handled over 9,000 consultations. Currently, the organization is treating some 2,500 patients and has a high rate of success with a variety of treatment approaches.

In addition to recovery treatments, ALUBA focuses on prevention, early detection and health education. In the schools, ALUBA's activities focus on the population at risk through consciousness-raising initiatives with teachers and parents. Special programs—group discussions, seminars and workshops—train families to prevent anorexia and bulimia and to detect symptoms of eating disorders early on, so that sufferers can receive prompt treatment.

Teachers Are Key

Because teachers are key to identifying pathological behavior in the school setting, ALUBA trains teachers through a specially-designed course in early detection.

The family is the focus of "health education" programs

which emphasize the importance of healthy relationships among family members. Order and mutual respect are prioritized, as are clear, well-defined roles within the family.

Many businesses dedicate time and resources to employees' family welfare, and ALUBA offers these companies prevention programs similar to those offered in the schools. Special explanatory pamphlets, videos and educational materials have been prepared for these activities.

While anorexia nervosa and bulimia are difficult to detect because those who suffer from eating disorders refuse to recognize that they are ill and hide their symptoms. The following are some danger signals.

If parents observe several of these characteristics in a child, a diagnostic consultation may be in order.

In the schools, teachers should take an interest in the issue and collaborate with the families in early detection. Their role is fundamental in the formation of young people free from addictions and prepared to face the challenges of life. For this reason, teachers must be properly informed about eating disorders. If we are able to train them, we strengthen the action of the family in the daily struggle against this scourge. We must therefore re-evaluate the role of teachers in prevention and early detection.

The following are some aspects to which teachers should be attentive:

Eating During Recess

Recess is a break to allow the students to rest and recover their energies in order to continue their activities. During this time to "recharge their batteries," students should eat appropriate food that assures their normal growth and good scholastic performance. The first red light for eating disorders among students is inappropriate eating habits during recess.

Physical Activity and Sports

Encouraging physical activity is healthy, but care should be taken: hyperactivity is one of the symptoms of an eating disorder. When exercise is practiced for the sole purpose of losing weight, in an intense and compulsive fashion and in prolonged sessions, this physical activity is not beneficial but rather activates the illness.

Perfectionism

We pay attention to exemplary students. We admire their work, their dedication to their studies, their habits. They are an example for the rest of the class. But when perfectionism is evident at every moment, this is characteristic of individuals suffering from anorexia.

Teachers should ask themselves: Are they obsessive about their physical appearance? Do they take great pains to have a "perfect" body? What are their eating habits? What are their physical activities?

Changes in Personality

Individuals with eating disorders display aggressive behavior, rage, crying jags, mood swings and withdrawal. If we notice these changes, we should look for other symptoms.

"Ugly Duckling Syndrome"

Low self-esteem and lack of faith in one's ability to succeed lead adolescents to see themselves as "losers." This "ugly duckling syndrome" is characteristic of both anorexia nervosa and bulimia.

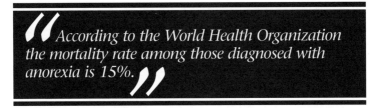

According to the World Health Organization the mortality rate among those diagnosed with anorexia is 15%.

Let's prevent the appearance of eating disorders. Let's encourage students to believe in themselves. Let's teach them to trust in their own abilities.

Values

Our culture admires power, money and the body beautiful above other values that are gradually being lost. If we stop to listen to students' conversations, we hear talk of "miracle diets" or "a great way to lose weight." We should encourage them to focus on other interests, providing an incentive to change and to abandon the fight for the "physical ideal."

Lack of Concentration

Occasionally the performance of a good student may waver; they can't seem to concentrate; and sometimes appear to drift off. Anorexia nervosa and bulimia lock their victims into a minute world in which the only things that matter are weight, calories, the scale and the diet; there is no room for other projects and interests.

Feeling Ashamed of Their Bodies

Because of their distorted body image, students who suffer eating disorders see themselves as "fat" even though they may be a normal weight or even under-weight. They generally try to hide their bodies, to escape the observation of others. They hide in oversized clothes; they refuse to use bathing suits; and they avoid any situations that would force them to show themselves.

Bathroom Use

Among the various methods for eliminating food, self-induced vomiting is one of the most frequent. Special attention should be paid to this behavior, especially after students eat during recess.

Teachers should observe this sort of behavior very carefully because the consequences of self-induced vomiting are very serious. Vomiting can cause decreased levels of potassium in the blood, which can cause heart attacks.

Teachers who become aware of this issue, understand it and collaborate in prevention and early detection of anorexia nervosa and bulimia in the schools are our strongest allies in the struggle against these terrible disorders.

Profile of the Anorexic Patient

- Lack of awareness of the illness
- Intense fear of obesity
- Distorted self-image (they see themselves as fat even though they are under-weight)
- Refusal to maintain normal weight
- Hair loss
- Amenorrhea (lack of menstruation)
- Dry skin
- Hypertension
- Hypothermia

- Habit of cutting food in small bites
- Tendency to eat slowly
- Tendency to chew for a long time
- Preference for small portions
- Habit of spitting out, throwing away or hiding food
- Use of anorexic agents, laxatives and/or diuretics
- Habitual calorie counting
- Rituals revolving around food
- Hyper-activity to lose weight
- Social isolation
- Irritability
- Depression (present in 40–45% of all cases)
- Obsessive behavior
- High demand placed on self
- Rejection of sexuality
- Bingeing
- Use of loose clothing (which hides body)

3

Experiences of a Female Anorexic

Christy Heitger-Casbon

Christy Heitger-Casbon is a writer and editor for Serve, a regional educational laboratory that works to improve learning opportunities for all students. She is also a freelance writer on health and fitness, adolescence, and women's issues.

Some young girls believe that being thin is the key to beauty and popularity. I began to starve myself when I was a young girl in an effort to lose weight and gain friends. Unfortunately, my obsessive desire for thinness triggered anorexia. I was hospitalized until I began to eat again, and I started to recover. The feelings behind my anorexia led me to engage in other obsessive behaviors, however, such as excessive exercising. I have recovered from anorexia and compulsive exercising, but I must remain alert to the start of obsessive behaviors if I am to maintain a healthy lifestyle.

A healthy, balanced, satisfying life is what we all want, isn't it? We bone up on the latest research about nutrition and fitness, buy top-of-the-line health products and exercise equipment and attend the best time management seminars all in hopes of becoming the best we can be. Most of us have such wholesome, sincere, unadulterated intentions. Carrying them out in a healthy manner, however, is a different story. It's often not for lack of trying. It's quite the opposite, actually.

There are those of us who go to extremes in an intense effort to achieve the pinnacle of health. However, when you take things to the extreme, that is precisely when you get yourself into trouble. If you eat too much or too little, you feel ill. If you sleep too much or too little, you feel sluggish, if you exercise too much or too little, you harm your body both physically and psychologically. I know because I used to be one of those determined people who took things to the extreme. I still advocate exercise and nutrition, but I don't go overboard anymore because I learned the "lesson of moderation" the hard way.

My Anorexic Nightmare

My story began 14 years ago, when I was 12 years old. I was an awkward middle-schooler who desperately wanted to be beautiful and ached to be popular. It was clear from environmental influences (e.g., peers family and media) that obesity was not acceptable. I heard enough derogatory "fat" comments and witnessed enough pointed fingers while growing up to know that I didn't ever want to be shunned and ridiculed like that. Therefore, I came to the conclusion that to be beautiful and popular, you needed to be thin. Consequently, I started dieting, but I took it to the extreme. Within a three-month period, I had developed anorexia nervosa (a disorder characterized by a preoccupation with thinness and an extremely restrictive diet). Over the course of the summer, I dropped from 110 pounds to a skeletal 73 pounds.

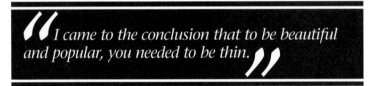

I came to the conclusion that to be beautiful and popular, you needed to be thin.

It's hard to believe that at the tender age of 12 I had already headed down a destructive, devastating and addictive path. People may not think of anorexia as an addiction, but in many ways it is. Experts maintain that all addictions are the pursuit or avoidance of a feeling. As a teenager, I wanted to avoid feeling self-hatred and disgust. I grew tired of looking at myself and being repulsed by what I saw in the mirror, so I starved myself in an attempt to drop pounds and pick up friends. I convinced myself that if I were thin, I'd be accepted and liked by those around me. My ambition backfired, however. Instead of gaining a social network of friends, I landed in an isolated hospital room. Instead of feeling thin, beautiful and popular, I felt grotesque, awkward and lonely. Over the course of the next few years, I received therapy. Throughout my teenage years, I slowly gained weight—ounce by ounce, pound by pound. Three years later, I had returned to a healthy weight. Of course, that didn't mean I had fully recovered psychologically. I still had very low self-confidence, and building that would take a long time.

Running for My Life

I needed to find a way to feel good about myself without falling back into the starvation pattern again, but I didn't quite know how to do that. I started by turning my attention toward something positive rather than negative, focusing on my health rather than my weight. For years, I'd been so preoccupied with the numbers on the scale, I couldn't move beyond that. I wanted to find a way to eat without being terrified of getting fat. Needless to say, this process was arduous and frustrating. For one thing, starving myself for so long had royally screwed up my metabolism. Therefore, I couldn't eat as much as the average woman because my metabolism was so slow. I wanted to find a safe way to give it a boost. I'd read about how exercise helps maintain muscle mass and how this conservation of muscle is important in maintaining a normal metabolic rate. Therefore, I decided to give exercise a try.

I can still recall the first half-mile loop around my neighborhood. Boy, was I pathetic. I was a determined teenager, though, and vowed to persevere. For weeks, I huffed and puffed and absolutely hated lacing up my shoes for my two-mile run. One day, about six months later, I realized, "Hey, I'm actually enjoying this!" Before I knew it, an enthusiastic runner was born.

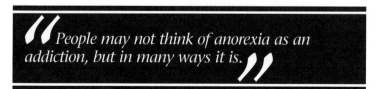

People may not think of anorexia as an addiction, but in many ways it is.

Running produced a wide range of physical and psychological benefits. Sometimes, I'd catch myself thinking, "Wow, who knew that I could find a fun activity that actually reduces my risk of heart disease and osteoporosis?" I also periodically took my resting heart rate when I first woke up in the morning because I found it amusing to count my heartbeats and knew

26   *At Issue*

that as I continued to condition my body, my heart muscle was getting stronger, as were other parts of my body. My lung capacity increased and even the steepest hills didn't leave me breathless anymore. One of the best things ever—especially from a former anorexic's point of view—was to look in a mirror at the body I had loathed for so many years and be able to recognize that it had blossomed into a strong, muscular, curvaceous one. Running definitely gave me the gift of life. Three years ago, however, I began abusing that gift when I started exercising compulsively.

A Few Just Wouldn't Do

When I had anorexia, I found that the more I limited my food intake, the better I felt. This may sound strange, but studies have shown starvation actually alters brain chemistry. Under-eating can activate brain chemicals that produce feelings of peace and euphoria. Some researchers believe that anorexics use the restriction of food to self-medicate painful feelings and distressing moods.

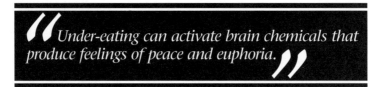

Under-eating can activate brain chemicals that produce feelings of peace and euphoria.

Years later, I subconsciously did the same thing running. I relied on my workouts to suppress and alter my negative emotions. When I first began running, I ran four or five days a week and jogged approximately 20 miles weekly. For seven years, I slowly increased my mileage but still maintained a safe, normal, healthy exercise regimen. It was only when I became addicted to exercise that my behavior turned unhealthy.

I first realized I had a problem when one day, three years ago, I freaked out at the prospect of taking a day off from exercise. My husband and I were in Indiana over Christmas break and a blizzard hit town. Even after the storm subsided, I couldn't run outside because there was blowing and drifting snow. I couldn't get to a gym, either, because the roads were closed. On top of that, my in-laws didn't own a treadmill. When I realized that I had no way of exercising that day, I flipped out. My mind was racing as I desperately tried to figure out an alternative way to run. When I couldn't find a solution, I was overcome by a paralyzing fear. It was so surreal.

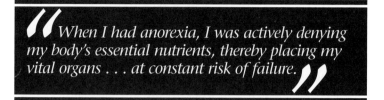

When I had anorexia, I was actively denying my body's essential nutrients, thereby placing my vital organs . . . at constant risk of failure.

I thought to myself, "Taking a day off is something I used to do and was fine with. Why does it terrify me now? And what am I afraid of, anyway?" I couldn't explain or rationalize my emotions. All I knew was that I felt completely trapped and amazingly anxious—feelings that only increased with time. In the height of my compulsive exercise addiction, I painstakingly scheduled business meetings and personal vacations around my running regimen. In 1995, I even scheduled the time of my wedding around my daily run. I knew this wasn't normal, yet I couldn't change my behavior.

Risky Business

My running routine didn't become a problem until I let it consume and control me. Just as my moderate exercise routine had originally produced numerous benefits, my excessive running routine produced numerous problems. I experienced knee pain, hip pain, ankle pain, muscle cramps, headaches, shin splints and pulled muscles, but the discomfort was never enough to prompt me to cut back on my workouts. Despite the fact these pains were a direct result of my compulsive running, I chose to overlook the adverse consequences and continued to run. . . .

When I had anorexia, I was actively denying my body's essential nutrients, thereby placing my vital organs (i.e., heart, lungs, kidneys) at constant risk of failure. However, no matter the risks, I stubbornly refused to eat. I understood I needed to gain weight to stay alive, but found the actual process of lifting food to my lips too much to bear. Ultimately, I couldn't, wouldn't and didn't eat until I was hospitalized and forced to do so.

Everyone knows that excessively limiting food intake is dangerous, but recognizing excessive exercise as dangerous isn't quite as obvious because the signs aren't visible or evident. Nevertheless, the danger is just as real. Just as my old addiction had a name (anorexia), my new one did, too. Researchers call it "anorexia athletica" or "compulsive exercise," and its consequences are numerous. Anorexia Nervosa and Related Eating Disorders (ANRED) reports that the consequences of compulsive exercise include abandoned relationships, damaged careers, lower grades in school, stress fractures, as well as damaged bones, joints, and soft tissues. Some psychological effects include obsessive thoughts, compulsive behaviors, self-worth measured only in terms of performance, depression, guilt and anxiety when exercise is impossible. . . .

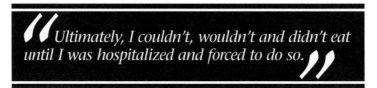

Ultimately, I couldn't, wouldn't and didn't eat until I was hospitalized and forced to do so.

Six months ago, after concluding that I wanted to be an "avid" runner rather than an "addicted" one, I altered my exercise regimen. I began by slowly reducing my mileage and adding cross-training activities such as weightlifting, biking, swimming and tennis. Then, I started taking two "rest" days a week. Admittedly, allowing myself rest days was not easy to do. As strange as it sounds, for a while, I felt guilty for getting hungry on days I hadn't exercised. My first inclination was to cut back on my food intake on my rest days. Nancy Clark, M.S., R.D., author of *Nancy Clark's Sports Nutrition Guidebook*, warns against this because, as she says, "Your muscles will be busy replacing glycogen stores with the carbohydrates you normally burn off during exercise."

I've actually grown to appreciate my rest days because I don't view them as lazy, inactive days, but rather as free, unstructured ones. On these days, I'll take long evening walks with my husband or swim a few easy laps in the pool to unwind. It just depends on what I feel like doing.

Psychological and Physical Benefits

I've noticed both psychological and physical benefits as a result of my new, balanced approach to health and fitness. Psychologically, I feel much healthier since I began exercising in moderation. Now that every second of my day doesn't revolve around my workout, I enjoy life more. I know that I'll get my workout in because I'm still an enthusiastic and motivated individual, but I don't let obsessive thoughts about exercise consume me anymore. For example, if something comes up and I have to push my workout back a couple of hours, it's not a big deal. (I couldn't have said that a year ago.) . . .

I've lived so much of my life in fear of things—fear of getting fat, fear of losing control, fear of what others think of me, fear of failure and fear of disappointing others. However, I've let go of all that. Fear and obsession no longer rule my life. I'm finally living a healthy, sensible and balanced lifestyle.

4

Experiences of a Male Anorexic

Thomas Holbrook

Thomas Holbrook is a psychiatrist and clinical director of the Eating Disorders Program at Rogers Memorial Hospital in Oconomowoc, Wisconsin.

My eating disorder began when I had to stop running due to knee problems. I started obsessing about my weight—afraid that I would get fat since I was no longer engaged in strenuous exercise—and began cutting calories. Over a ten year period, I slipped deeper into anorexia and was hospitalized several times. No one ever questioned my eating habits or diagnosed my anorexia. I believe that this is because I am a man and anorexia is associated with women. Ultimately, I diagnosed myself and began treatment. Even then, many of my colleagues had difficulty believing that I—a man—was anorexic. After extensive therapy, I have successfully recovered from anorexia.

In the spring of 1976, two years into my psychiatric practice, I began having pain in both knees, which soon severely limited my running. I was advised by an orthopedist to stop trying to run through the pain. After many failed attempts to treat the condition with orthotic surgery and physical therapy, I resigned myself to giving up running. As soon as I made that decision, the fear of gaining weight and getting fat consumed me. I started weighing myself every day, and even though I was not gaining weight, I started feeling fatter. I became increasingly obsessed about my energy balance and whether I was burning off the calories I consumed. I refined my knowledge of nutrition and memorized the calories and grams of fat, protein, and carbohydrates of every food I would possibly eat.

Despite what my intellect told me, my goal became to rid my body of all fat. I resumed exercising. I found I could walk good distances, despite some discomfort, if I iced my knees afterward. I started walking several times a day. I built a small pool in my basement and swam in place, tethered to the wall. I biked as much as I could tolerate. The denial of what I only much later came to recognize as anorexia involved overuse injuries as I sought medical help for tendonitis, muscle and joint pain, and entrapment neuropathies. I was never told that I was exercising too much, but I am sure that had I been told, I would not have listened.

Worst Nightmare

Despite my efforts, my worst nightmare was happening. I felt and saw myself as fatter than ever before, even though I had started to lose weight. Whatever I had learned about nutrition in medical school or read in books, I perverted to my purpose. I obsessed about protein and fat. I increased the number of egg whites that I ate a day to 12. If any yolk leaked into my concoction of egg whites, Carnation Instant Breakfast, and skim milk, I threw the entire thing out.

As I became more restrictive, caffeine became more and more important and functional for me. It staved off my appetite, although I didn't let myself think about it that way. Coffee and soda perked me up emotionally and focused my thinking. I really do not believe that I could have continued to function at work without caffeine.

> *Despite what my intellect told me, my goal became to rid my body of all fat.*

I relied equally on my walking (up to six hours a day) and restrictive eating to fight fat, but it seemed I could never walk far enough or eat little enough. The scale was now the final analysis of everything about me. I weighed myself before and after every meal and walk. An increase in weight meant I had not tried hard enough and needed to walk farther or on steeper hills, and eat less. If I lost weight, I was encouraged and all the more determined to eat less and exercise more. However, my goal was not to be thinner, just not fat. I still wanted to be "big and strong"—just not fat.

Ritualistic Eating

Besides the scale, I measured myself constantly by assessing how my clothes fit and felt on my body. I compared myself to other people, using this information to "keep me on track." As I had when I compared myself to others in terms of intelligence, talent, humor, and personality, I fell short in all categories. All of those feelings were channeled into the final "fat equation."

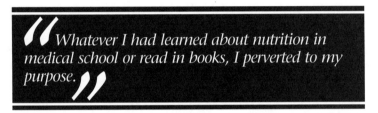

Whatever I had learned about nutrition in medical school or read in books, I perverted to my purpose.

During the last few years of my illness, my eating became more extreme. My meals were extremely ritualistic, and by the time I was ready for dinner, I had not eaten all day and had exercised five or six hours. My suppers became a relative binge. I still thought of them as "salads," which satisfied my anorexic mind. They evolved from just a few different types of lettuce and some raw vegetables and lemon juice for dressing to rather elaborate concoctions. I must have been at least partly aware that my muscles were wasting away because I made a point of adding protein, usually in the form of tuna fish. I added other foods from time to time in a calculated and compulsive way. Whatever I added, I had to continue with, and usually in increasing amounts. A typical binge might consist of a head of iceberg lettuce, a full head of raw cabbage, a defrosted package of frozen spinach, a can of tuna, garbanzo beans, croutons, sunflower seeds, artificial bacon bits, a can of pineapple, lemon juice, and vinegar, all in a foot-and-a-half-wide bowl. In my phase of eating carrots, I would eat about a pound of raw carrots while I was preparing the salad. The raw cabbage was my laxative. I counted on that control over my bowels for added reassurance that the food was not staying in my body long enough to make me fat.

The final part of my ritual was a glass of cream sherry. Although I obsessed all day about my binge, I came to depend on the relaxing effect of the sherry. My long-standing insomia worsened as my eating became more disordered, and I became dependent on the soporific effect of alcohol. When I was not in too much physical discomfort from the binge, the food and alcohol would put me to sleep, but only for about four hours or so. I awoke at 2:30 or 3:00 A.M. and started my walks. It was always in the back of my mind that I would not be accruing fat if I wasn't sleeping. And, of course, moving was always better than not. Fatigue also helped me modify the constant anxiety I felt. Over-the-counter cold medications, muscle relaxants, and Valium also gave me relief from my anxiety. The combined effect of medication with low blood sugar was relative euphoria.

Oblivious to Illness

While I was living this crazy life, I was carrying on my psychiatric practice, much of which consisted of treating eating-disordered patients—anorexic, bulimic, and obese. It is incredible to me now that I could be working with anorexic patients who were not any sicker than I was, even healthier in some ways, and yet remain completely oblivious to my own illness. There were only extremely brief flashes of insight. If I happened to see myself in a mirrored window reflection, I would be horrified at how emaciated I appeared. Turning away, the insight was gone. I was well aware of my usual self-doubts and insecurities, but that was normal for me. Unfortunately, the increasing spaciness that I was experiencing with weight loss and minimal nutrition was also becoming "normal" for me. In fact, when I was at my spaciest, I felt the best, because it meant that I was not getting fat.

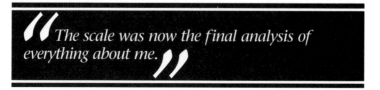

The scale was now the final analysis of everything about me.

Only occasionally would a patient comment on my appearance. I would blush, feel hot, and sweat with shame but not recognize cognitively what he or she was saying. More surprising to me, in retrospect, was never having been confronted about my eating or weight loss by the professionals with whom I worked all during this time. I remember a physician administrator of the hospital kidding me occasionally about eating so little, but I was never seriously questioned about my eating, weight loss, or exercise. They all must have seen me out walking for an hour or two every day regardless of the weather. I even had a down-filled body suit that I would put over my work clothes, allowing me to walk no matter how low the temperature. My work must have suffered during these years, but I did not notice or hear about it.

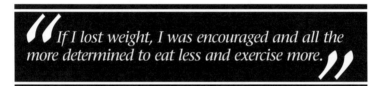

If I lost weight, I was encouraged and all the more determined to eat less and exercise more.

People outside of work seemed relatively oblivious as well. Family registered concern about my overall health and the various physical problems I was having but were apparently completely unaware of the connection with my eating and weight loss, poor nutrition, and excessive exercise. I was never exactly gregarious, but my social isolation became extreme in my illness. I declined social invitations as much as I could. This included family gatherings. If I accepted an invitation that would include a meal, I would either not eat or bring my own food. During those years, I was virtually friendless.

ER Visits Yield No Diagnosis

I still find it hard to believe that I was so blind to the illness, especially as a physician aware of the symptoms of anorexia nervosa. I could see my weight dropping but could only believe it was good, despite conflicting thoughts about it. Even when I started feeling weak and tired, I did not understand. As I experienced the progressive physical sequelae of my weight loss, the picture only grew murkier. My bowels stopped functioning normally, and I developed severe abdominal cramping and diarrhea. In addition to the cabbage, I was sucking on packs of sugarless candies, sweetened with Sorbitol to diminish hunger and for its laxative effect. At my worst, I was spending up to a couple of hours a day in the bathroom. In the winter I had severe Raynaud's Phenomenon, during which all the digits on my hands and feet would become white and excruciatingly painful. I was dizzy and lightheaded. Severe back spasms occurred occasionally, resulting in a number of ER visits by ambulance. I was asked no questions and no diagnosis was made despite my physical appearance and low vital signs.

Around this time I was recording my pulse down into the 30s. I remember thinking that this was good because it meant that I was "in shape." My skin was paper thin. I became increasingly tired during the day and would find myself almost dozing off while in sessions with patients. I was short of breath at times and would feel my heart pound. One night I was shocked to discover that I had pitting edema of both legs up to my knees. Also around that time, I fell while ice skating and bruised my knee. The swelling was enough to tip the cardiac balance, and I passed out. More trips to the ER and several admissions to the hospital for assessment and stabilization still resulted in no diagnosis. Was it because I was a man?

I was finally referred to the Mayo Clinic with the hope of identifying some explanation for my myriad of symptoms. During the week at Mayo, I saw almost every kind of specialist and was tested exhaustively. However, I was never questioned about my eating or exercise habits. They only remarked that I had an extremely high carotene level and that my skin was certainly orangish (this was during one of my phases of high carrot consumption). I was told that my problems were "functional," or, in other words, "in my head," and that they probably stemmed from my father's suicide 12 years earlier.

Physician, Heal Thyself

An anorexic woman with whom I had been working for a couple of years finally reached me when she questioned whether she could trust me. At the end of a session on a Thursday, she asked for reassurance that I would be back on Monday and continue to work with her. I replied that, of course, I would be back, "I don't abandon my patients."

She said, "My head says yes, but my heart says no." After attempting to reassure her, I did not give it a second thought until Saturday morning, when I heard her words again.

I was staring out my kitchen window, and I started experiencing deep feelings of shame and sadness. For the first time I recognized that I was anorexic, and I was able to make sense of what had happened to me over the last 10 years. I could identify all the symptoms of anorexia that I knew so well in my patients. While this was a relief, it was also very frightening. I felt alone and terrified of what I knew I had to do—let other people know that I was anorexic. I had to eat and stop exercising compulsively. I had no idea if I could really do it—I had been this way for so long. I could not imagine what recovery would be like or how I could possibly be okay without my eating disorder.

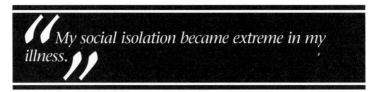

My social isolation became extreme in my illness.

I was afraid of the responses that I would get. I was doing individual and group therapy with mostly eating-disordered patients in two inpatient programs, one for young adults (ages 12 to 22) and the other for older adults. For some reason, I was more anxious about the younger group. My fears proved unfounded. When I told them that I was anorexic, they were as accepting and supportive of me and my illness as they were of one another. There was more of a mixed response from hospital staff. One of my colleagues heard about it and suggested that my restrictive eating was merely a "bad habit" and that I could not *really* be anorexic. Some of my coworkers were immediately supportive; others seemed to prefer not to talk about it.

That Saturday I knew what I was facing. I had a fairly good idea of what I would have to change. I had no idea how slow the process would be or how long it would take. With the dropping of my denial, recovery became a possibility and gave me some direction and purpose outside of the structure of my eating disorder.

Supper Was the Easiest Meal

The eating was slow to normalize. It helped to start thinking of eating three meals a day. My body needed more than I could eat in three meals, but it took me a long time to be comfortable eating snacks. Grain, protein, and fruit were the easiest food groups to eat consistently. Fat and dairy groups took much longer to include. Supper continued to be my easiest meal and breakfast came easier than lunch. It helped to eat meals out. I was never really safe just cooking for myself. I started eating breakfast and lunch at the hospital where I worked and eating suppers out.

During my marital separation and for a few years after the divorce from my first wife, my children spent weekdays with their mother and weekends with me. Eating was easier when I was taking care of them because I simply had to have food around for them. I met and courted my second wife during this time, and by the time we were married, my son Ben was in college and my daughter Sarah was applying to go. My second wife enjoyed cooking and would cook supper for us. This was the first time since high school that I had had suppers prepared for me.

After ten years in recovery, my eating now seems second nature to me. Although I still have occasional days of feeling fat and still have a tendency to choose foods lower in fat and calories, eating is relatively easy because I go ahead and eat what I need. During more difficult times I still think of it in terms of what I *need to eat*, and I will even carry on a brief inner dialogue about it.

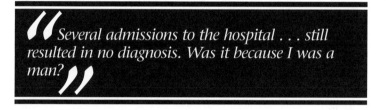

Several admissions to the hospital . . . still resulted in no diagnosis. Was it because I was a man?

My second wife and I divorced awhile back, but it is still hard to shop for food and cook by myself. Eating out is safe for me now, however. I will sometimes order the special, or the same selection that someone else is ordering as a way of staying safe and letting go of my control over the food.

Toning Down

While I worked on my eating, I struggled to stop exercising compulsively. This proved much harder to normalize than the eating. Because I was eating more, I had a stronger drive to exercise to cancel calories. But the drive to exercise seemed also to have deeper roots. It was relatively easy to see how including several fats at a meal was something I needed to do to recover from this illness. But it was harder to reason in the same way for exercise. Experts talk about separating it from the illness and somehow preserving it for the obvious benefits of health and enjoyment. Even this is tricky. I enjoy exercise even when I am obviously doing it excessively. . . .

Being Oneself

One of the most significant insights I've gained in my recovery has been that I have spent my whole life trying to be somebody I'm not. Just like so many of my patients, I had the feeling that I was never good enough. In my own estimation, I was a failure. Any compliments or recognition of achievement did not fit. On the contrary, I always expected to be "found out"—that others would discover that I was stupid, and it would be all over. Always starting with the premise that who I am is not good enough, I have gone to such extremes to improve what I assumed needed improvement. My eating disorder was one of those extremes. It blunted my anxieties and gave me a false sense of security through the control over food, body shape, and weight. My recovery has allowed me to experience these same anxieties and insecurities without the necessity of escape through control over food. . . .

I have not had to change in the ways that I initially feared. I have let myself respect the interests and feelings that I have always had. I can experience my fears without needing to escape.

5

Anorexia Occurs Among African Americans

Shannah Tharp-Taylor

Shannah Tharp-Taylor is a staff reporter for the Chicago Tribune.

Black women often suffer needlessly from anorexia because doctors do not expect to find eating disorders in the African American community and thus misdiagnose their anorexic patients. It has been thought that the African American community's greater acceptance of larger body sizes for women offers black teens some protection against anorexia. However, as African Americans take on the cultural values of the mainstream—white—culture, any protection provided by greater acceptance of diverse body types has diminished. While more research on eating disorders in minorities is needed, it appears that anorexia depends more on socioeconomic status than on race.

In many ways, Stephanie Doswell is your regular college student in a T-shirt and flare-legged jeans. But she is also anorexic, bulimic and African-American, a combination so rare that it sometimes goes unrecognized.

"If someone sees a sickly, thin white person, they automatically think that they have anorexia," said Doswell, 19. "If someone sees a sickly, thin black person, they don't think that they have anorexia."

She adds sarcastically: "Because blacks don't get anorexia."

While their numbers are probably small, black anorexics face a host of unique problems, including inadequate diagnoses from doctors not expecting to find eating disorders in African-Americans.

Anorexia has been thought of as a disease affecting rich, white females since the 1940s because it primarily affects girls from well-to-do Caucasian families.

Recent studies seem to confirm that black anorexics are extremely hard to find. Last month [July 2003] Ruth Striegel-Moore of Wesleyan University in Connecticut reported in the *American Journal of Psychiatry* that although anorexia is believed to affect 1 percent to 2 percent of the general population, none of the 1,061 young black women in their study was anorexic.

But many experts doubt that black anorexics are as rare as studies have suggested, though experts are left guessing at how prevalent the disease is in minorities.

Traditionally, African-American girls have been thought to have some protection from eating disorders such as anorexia nervosa and bulimia nervosa because of a greater acceptance of larger body size in the African-American community, said Gayle Brooks, an African-American psychologist specializing in eating disorders at the Renfrew Center in Florida.

Gaps in Knowledge

But this alleged protection from eating disorders appears to weaken as blacks take on the values of the mainstream culture, Brooks says.

"I think that there are a lot of African-American women who are really struggling with their sense of personal identity and self-esteem that comes with being a part of this culture that does not accept who we really are," Brooks said.

Black anorexics face a host of unique problems, including inadequate diagnoses from doctors not expecting to find eating disorders in African-Americans.

For years anorexia (characterized by refusal to eat enough) and bulimia (characterized by binge eating and purging) was only studied in white females, leaving gaps in medical knowledge about eating disorders and how they affect minorities.

For example, experts are not sure whether black girls from high-income families are more likely than their poorer counterparts to develop eating disorders, as is believed to be the case for white girls.

Striegel-Moore acknowledges that her study may have underestimated the number of blacks with anorexia nervosa because she had too few girls from affluent black families.

Many experts doubt that black anorexics are as rare as studies have suggested.

Similarly, psychologists typically search for anorexia in adolescents, the age group commonly found to have the disorder in white girls. However, experts question whether anorexia may develop later in African-Americans.

Thomas Joiner, a professor of psychology at Florida State University, tested whether racial stereotypes influence the recognition of eating disorders. He asked 150 people to read a fictional diary of a 16-year-old girl named Mary and rated whether they thought the girl had an eating disorder.

For some the diary was labeled "Mary, 16-year-old Caucasian." For others it was labeled "Mary, 16-year-old African-American."

More people said the subject had an eating disorder when she was labeled white than when she was labeled black.

"Race mattered," Joiner said. "There's the idea in people's minds that African-American girls tend not to get eating disorders. And that influenced their judgments."

Joiner and his colleagues also found that many health care professionals were unable to recognize black anorexics, suggesting that could contribute to missed diagnoses.

"(Doctors) should have their same radar out for eating disorders when talking with an African-American girl as when they are sitting across from Caucasian girls," Joiner said.

One 17-year-old African-American girl from Washington, D.C., said her doctors did not diagnose her properly, even though she has been purging since age 10 and at 5 foot 7 has weighed as little as 95 pounds.

"The doctors just thought I had a stomach thing. . . . They gave me antibiotics and rehydrated me and sent me home," said the girl, who replied to an e-mail request from the *Chicago Tri-bune* asking African-American anorexics to share their stories.

One's Social Group Is More Important than One's Race

Many researchers and clinicians studying anorexia nervosa say that becoming anorexic is less a factor of race and more a consideration of one's social group.

However, girls from poor families face an additional risk because they are not likely to be able to afford treatment, which can cost as much as $30,000 for a month of in-patient care.

Doswell typifies some of the issues surrounding anorexia in black women.

Her condition was verified through her therapist, Keitha Austin of Newport News, Va., who received written permission to confirm that Doswell is an African-American female with anorexia.

She starts each day with eight melon-flavored gummy rings.

"I don't want a booty like J. Lo, [Jennifer Lopez, a Latina pop star]" Doswell said. "I don't want to look like Beyonce [an African-American pop star] because she is fat."

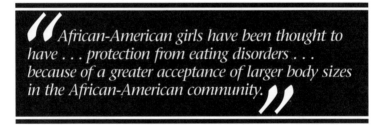

African-American girls have been thought to have . . . protection from eating disorders . . . because of a greater acceptance of larger body sizes in the African-American community.

Holidays at the Doswell home are filled with soul food, Doswell wrote in an e-mail interview. "Catfish, beans, collard greens. . . . Food is important to us," said Doswell, who describes her family as lower-middle class.

At 5 feet 4 inches tall—about average—Doswell weighs 93 pounds, less than 97 percent of women her age. She wears a size 3, she says, because she likes her clothes baggy.

Doswell said she envied her white, Hispanic and Asian friends, who were thin and preoccupied with weight.

Her roller coaster with eating disorders began in anticipation of an exchange program trip to Japan.

"I didn't want to be fat on the trip," Doswell said. "So, I

just stopped eating. It was that simple."

Thirteen pounds later, Doswell was still not happy with her new, thinner self. So she forced her weight lower into the upper 90s.

By spring 2002 she was eating only rice or fruit and exercising incessantly, stealing laxatives and throwing up the little food she consumed. But she did not know that her behaviors had a name.

Many health care professionals were unable to recognize black anorexics.

"I went online one day and found out that what I was doing was actually a disease," she said.

The Web has become a haven for young women with eating disorders who feel they have nowhere else to turn for help and support. The issue of race and stereotypes about eating disorders are hot topics for members of the Colours of Ana Web site, created as a support system for girls and women of color with anorexia and other eating disorders.

Many girls on the www.coloursofana.com site wrote that they have heard negative comments from other blacks suggesting that they developed anorexia because they are trying to be white by becoming thin.

"I have an eating disorder because I am sick, not because I am wanting to be white," wrote one woman. "We need to get past this sort of exclusivity. It is just not helping."

Race Is No Protection from Anorexia

In the mid-'80s Zina Garrison, a professional tennis star, looked around the tennis world and did not see anyone who looked like her.

"I didn't really have anyone to look up to," Garrison said in an interview. "At the time it was basically myself, Jackie Joyner-Kersee and Florence Joyner who were the pivotal African-American women athletes doing something."

At 21 years old, Garrison was ranked in the top 10 of women's tennis and had beaten Chris Evert. But still she struggled with self-image.

"I was in a short skirt all of the time, and I was always told that I didn't have the figure to fit the tennis skirts," Garrison said.

In an effort to fit the mold of the all-white world of women's tennis and the emptiness she felt as an athlete and public figure, Garrison tumbled into bulimic behavior without actually knowing that she was developing an eating disorder.

Purging took a toll on Garrison's health. Her hair started to fall out. Her skin became blotchy. Her nails softened.

Garrison became too weak to play the game she loved.

After watching a television show on bulimia and eating disorders, Garrison recognized her behavior as an illness, got help from her trainers and went on to return to the top of the tennis world as a winner of major tournaments.

Even now, Garrison said, "Recovery goes on day by day."

Kaelyn Carson was not as fortunate.

At 5 foot 8 and 115 pounds of solid muscle, Kaelyn Carson, of Comstock Park, Mich., was a brown-eyed beauty with long, curly brown hair and big dimples. But after a 14-month battle with anorexia and bulimia, Carson died at age 20. She weighed 75 pounds.

Carson, who was biracial—African American and white— exemplifies the fact that no one is immune from eating disorders because of her race.

"She was everything," said her mother, Brenda Carson.

But now she is left with only memories of her daughter, who was a member of the National Association of Collegiate Scholars, Miss Michigan American Teen, a cheerleader and a track star.

"Don't close your eyes to it," her mother said.

6

Anorexia Can Strike Older Women

Sabrina Rubin Erdely

Sabrina Rubin Erdely is a nationally known freelance writer whose work has appeared in many publications including Philadelphia Magazine, Glamour, *and* Redbook.

While the majority of Americans who suffer from eating disorders are under age twenty-five, an increasing number of women in their thirties and older are showing symptoms of anorexia. Psychiatrists maintain that the sources of stress in an adult woman's life are different—marriage, children, job—from that of a teen, but the response is the same: acute anxiety and stress. Thus, older women and teens both become anorexic in a misguided attempt to cope with stress and take control of a life that seems wildly out of control. Recovery from anorexia is often more difficult for adults than for teens, however, because most adults have responsibilities that cannot easily be put aside while they spend time in treatment centers. Also, adults must often return to the same stressful situations that triggered their anorexia. Learning new ways of coping with stress is the key to long-term adult recovery from anorexia.

Kathy Palmero woke up in the back of an ambulance. Foggily she tried to recall how she had gotten there. She lifted her head from the stretcher to look down at herself, at her thin body dressed in a too-big pantsuit. Oh, right. It was all coming back to her now. The 31-year-old sales executive had just returned to work after her lunch break. She had been sitting at her desk, chatting with a coworker. Then everything had gone black: Kathy had passed out cold. The embarrassing incident was just one more sign, Kathy felt, that her life was spinning out of control. The Pennsylvania resident had two colicky children under the age of 2 at home, who kept her awake all night with their fussing. Kathy's husband, Chris, was a state trooper who worked the night shift, so he couldn't offer her much help on that front. In fact, he and Kathy often saw each other only at dinnertime (Chris' breakfast) before he raced out the door. Worse, Kathy was still in emotional shambles after her mother's death six months before. With a demanding career added to the mix, the pressure had become too much.

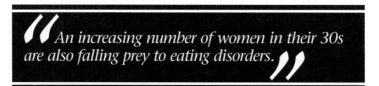

An increasing number of women in their 30s are also falling prey to eating disorders.

But in the midst of her private chaos, Kathy had discovered a way of managing her stress: She had all but ceased to eat. It began with fat-free foods and diet soda. Then her portions got smaller—and smaller. As the pounds flew off her five-foot-five, 168-pound frame, Kathy watched with pleasure as her curvy body transformed. Realizing that her rapid weight loss wasn't quite normal or healthy, Kathy never explained her strict regimen to anyone, offering only vague explanations to her friends and family about her increasingly slim physique.

Now, as Kathy's ambulance pulled up to the hospital, she cursed herself for allowing her secret to get out into the open. Sure enough, during a follow-up appointment a week later, Kathy's physician asked her whether she had been eating much. But by then, Kathy had her answer ready.

"Of course," she lied. Since Kathy wasn't drastically thin— at that point she weighed 120 pounds—the doctor believed her and sent her home. My secret's safe, Kathy said to herself with a sigh. Kathy, however, was anything but safe.

The Newest Victims of Eating Disorders

Anorexia and bulimia used to be ailments associated only with turbulent teenage years, and the majority of the five to ten million American sufferers are still under age 25.

But in a new phenomenon noticed by psychiatrists and

treatment centers, an increasing number of women in their 30s are also falling prey to eating disorders. "It's not just a teenage problem anymore," says Samuel E. Menaged, president of the Renfrew Center, the nation's largest eating-disorder facility. In the past, only a sprinkling of women over the age of 30 had sought inpatient help. But when the Renfrew staff looked at its 2003 roster, they realized that nearly a third of their residential patients were in this age group. At least half of them had suffered from eating disorders earlier in life; the other half were brand-new cases. "We're witnessing a very real shift," says William Davis, Ph.D., vice president of research and program development at Renfrew. "It's a trend that I suspect is going to continue to grow."

Whether you're 13 or 30, the main issue behind an eating disorder remains the same: It's a misguided way of coping with stress, a way of imposing control in your otherwise crazy life. But the stresses that can trigger an eating disorder in your 30s are very different from those that teens face. They tend to be uniquely adult concerns, ones that stem from the everyday juggling act of being a wife, a mother, and an employee—things like marital strain, job stress, child-rearing worries, and financial decisions.

> *Whether you're 13 or 30, the main issue behind an eating disorder remains the same: It's a misguided way of coping with stress.*

"Playing all those roles creates anxiety. All that anxiety makes women feel negative about themselves, because women tend to blame themselves instead of blaming the situation," observes Davis. "They can't say, 'I simply don't have time to get things done'; they say, 'What's wrong with me that I can't get things done?'"

And that self-doubt plays itself out against a charged backdrop: the societal pressure to be thin. For a woman in her 30s— who may be having babies, developing her first wrinkles, and noticing her slowing metabolism—it introduces yet another thing to worry about. "Women in our culture are bombarded with the notion that you have to be thin to be OK," says Davis. "So now you have women who are feeling vulnerable or troubled, and they are hitting on thinness as a solution to their problems as well as a sign that they're in charge of their lives."

The Role of Genetics

Of course, not every woman who's on a diet and has too much on her to-do list winds up with an eating disorder. The main factor that determines who's most vulnerable may be genetic: A study at UCLA found that female relatives of women with anorexia or bulimia are up to 12 times more likely to develop an eating disorder than women in unaffected families. Personality also plays a strong role. "Traits like perfectionism, anxiety, and a desire to please others are extremely common among people with eating disorders," adds Davis. That doesn't mean that everybody with such traits gets an eating disorder; it only means that those people, if exposed to a certain environment (for example, one that fosters low self-esteem or poor body image), are more likely to develop one.

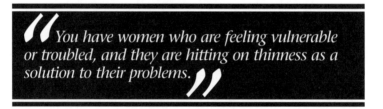

> *You have women who are feeling vulnerable or troubled, and they are hitting on thinness as a solution to their problems.*

Many sufferers, like Kathy Palmero, live for months or years in denial that they have an eating disorder. And even when they do realize that they're harming themselves, they tend to cling desperately to the comfort and sense of order that their anorexia or bulimia brings. For harried women who lack precious "me time," eating disorders can also represent something more. Since their activity of paring portions, bingeing and purging, or taking laxatives is something they engage in entirely alone—a private regimen or even a "pleasure" not performed for their husband or kids—they tend to view it as a cherished indulgence, a twisted logic that can make this disorder even harder to overcome.

When a Diet Gets Dangerous

For some women, eating disorders appear seemingly out of nowhere, overwhelming them even if they never had weight is-

sues as a teen. That was definitely the case with Kathy, who dieted occasionally during her youth but never in an unhealthy
way. "I was never fat, but I was always big-boned," Kathy says.
Outgoing Kathy learned to play her insecurity for laughs each
year she'd joke with her future husband, Chris, about how for
her birthday she wanted "anorexia, but only for a week."

"It was a big standing joke," she remembers.

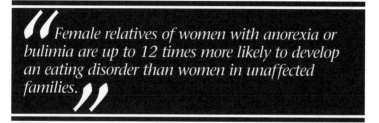

Female relatives of women with anorexia or bulimia are up to 12 times more likely to develop an eating disorder than women in unaffected families.

Life quickly changed for Kathy at 27, after she married
Chris. In rapid succession, she gave birth to her first child and
got pregnant again—and spent that pregnancy caring not only
for her infant son but also for her 55-year-old mother, who was
gravely ill with a brain tumor and died when Kathy was seven
months along. Adding to her devastation was the fact that
Chris, working odd hours, was almost never around. On top of
it all, Kathy's back-to-back pregnancies had saddled her with additional pounds. "You'll never be skinny again, not after two C-
sections," one coworker clucked. At 30, Kathy suddenly didn't
recognize her life anymore. "Before having kids I would go out
to dinner with friends. I had time with my husband, time to
myself," she says. "Two years later I woke up and I was a mom,
and my life had totally changed. I resented everything."

Kathy started losing weight from the stress, which robbed
her of her appetite. Thrilled with the results, Kathy decided to
go on a real diet. First she avoided anything with fat, drastically
reduced her portion sizes, and hid her skimpy meals from her
husband by pushing food around on her plate. Within six
months, Kathy lost 80 pounds. Still, she kept at it. "I couldn't
do anything about my mother's death, or my husband's job, or
the fact that my kids never slept," she says. "But my weight was
one thing I could control. And I did it well." At her thinnest,
Kathy weighed just 85 pounds.

Her husband was unaware of her problem for months, in
part because of their different schedules. One day, however,
when Chris caught sight of Kathy in her underwear, he freaked

out. "Jesus Christ, what happened to you?" he exclaimed. Kathy made a lot of excuses, and Chris didn't know what to believe— a common mistake among men who aren't taught to recognize the symptoms of an eating disorder. Kathy, in turn, was masterful at hiding her problem, as she had done with her doctor and her coworkers months earlier, when she fainted in her office.

Then one fateful day, Kathy's father came to visit—with his new girlfriend. Still mired in grief over her mother's death less than a year earlier, "that put me over the edge," she says. Overwhelmed with the need to purge, she excused herself to go to the bathroom, where she drank from a bottle of ipecac syrup and dry-heaved until she lost consciousness. Her 1½-year-old son eventually found her limp figure on the bathroom floor and called out for his dad. When Kathy finally awoke in the company of her worried husband and son, she knew she had hit rock bottom and decided to get help: "The fact that my son saw me like that, I thought, 'What the hell are you doing? If you keep this up, you won't be able to be a mother to your kids.'"

When Weight Is a Lifetime Struggle

While some women find themselves struggling with eating disorders for the first time in their lives as adults, for others, it's a more familiar battle: They experience the disorder as teens, then suffer relapses. . . .

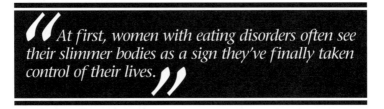

At first, women with eating disorders often see their slimmer bodies as a sign they've finally taken control of their lives.

At first, women with eating disorders often see their slimmer bodies as a sign they've finally taken control of their lives. But sooner or later, most come up against the harsh truth: that their disorder controls them, sometimes subtly forcing them to sacrifice the things that they normally hold dear. Janice Fingland, 38, knows this all too well. It started when, while trying to take some weight off her five-foot-one, 178-pound frame, she went on the Atkins diet and took a laxative to relieve her constipation. Thrilled the next day when she had lost two pounds, Janice started popping laxatives daily—and the pounds kept melting away. "I was getting compliments like crazy!" she says. "It was so flattering. I felt like I had finally taken charge of my looks."

Marital Problems

Then Janice began to look starved and unhealthy. Her shoulder blades began looking bony, her neck scrawny. When her second husband, Jeff, became suspicious, Janice broke down and confessed her laxative habit, and promised she would stop using the pills. As soon as she stopped, however, Janice swelled with water retention as her dehydrated body held on to every drop of fluid she consumed. Unable to button her jeans, Janice panicked. "I didn't want to get fat again," she says. Janice threw herself back into her disorder, secretly cutting her daily meal plan down to just one salad—plus 30 laxatives, an all-time high.

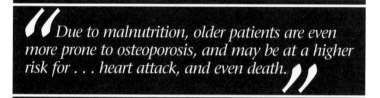

Due to malnutrition, older patients are even more prone to osteoporosis, and may be at a higher risk for . . . heart attack, and even death.

Jeff realized that his wife had returned to her self-destructive habits and researched therapists for her to consult, but she refused to call one. As her weight dropped to 100 pounds, Jeff finally gave Janice an ultimatum. "He was pushing me to get help, and I didn't want to. So we separated," Janice says, sounding as if she can hardly believe it herself. "I chose the laxatives over my own husband." Janice was numb the day Jeff packed and left. He told her that he would return when she decided to seek treatment.

Janice's daughters, then a 13-year-old and 10-year-old twins, were confused about their stepfather's sudden absence and why their mom seemed increasingly removed. She was exhausted, depressed, and sometimes racked with chest pains, which can occur in women with eating disorders. Nine months after Jeff moved out—and after having lived with anorexia for three years—Janice knew she couldn't go on much longer. "I saw my life crumbling before me," she recalls. "I stopped bonding with my kids. I had pushed my husband out of the house and didn't even know why. I knew I wasn't happy. Finally I said, 'I'm done. I need help.'"

She made two calls: one to her therapist and one to her husband, who moved back home a few weeks later, after she showed him that she was serious about beating her disorder. "Jeff had been through Alcoholics Anonymous 15 years before, so he knew that until I was ready to get help, I'd push everybody away," she says. "So he let me go—but also let me know that he'd be there when I was ready to say, 'I can't do this anymore.'"

The Long Road to Recovery

Admitting to having anorexia or bulimia can be hard for anyone. But it can be particularly hard for women who are used to keeping it all together. However, acknowledging the problem and getting help is especially crucial for adults, whose bodies don't bounce back as easily as a teen's will, emphasizes Davis. Due to malnutrition, older patients are even more prone to osteoporosis, and may be at a higher risk for respiratory infections, kidney failure, heart attack, and even death.

Another hurdle women face in getting treatment is that most sufferers require inpatient therapy for weeks on end, a time-out few women can manage as easily as a teenager can. . . .

Eventually, . . . Janice and Kathy sought residential treatment, which involves weeks of one-on-one therapy in a facility to teach patients alternate ways of coping with stress. Janice, for example, learned to be more open with her husband and others about her feelings: "I used to keep everything inside. Now if something is bothering me, I'll tell them and it'll help me get my mind off things." During treatment, patients also participate in group therapy, which shows them that they're not alone. . . .

The hardest part . . . isn't the treatment: It's how patients deal afterward.

But the hardest part, say experts, isn't the treatment: It's how patients deal afterward. Even though there is research to suggest that after eight to ten years many women with eating disorders recover, a great many people continue to suffer, according to Davis. Returning to reality can be especially tough for adults, because the demands of family and work life constantly threaten to draw them back into their unhealthy patterns. "It's a more difficult transition," says Davis. "The equilibrium in a marriage or a family has been disrupted, so you're going back to a lot of tension about what things are going to be like at home." Returning to work can be just as daunting. "They often worry about being fired or of no longer being seen as competent," says Davis.

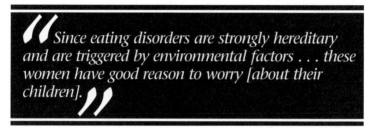

Since eating disorders are strongly hereditary and are triggered by environmental factors . . . these women have good reason to worry [about their children].

Kathy, for one, had a difficult time bridging the gap between her month-long inpatient treatment and the real world. "If I gained weight, ate something I shouldn't have eaten, or I had a day when I didn't feel like I had accomplished anything, it would set me back," Kathy recalls. Mere weeks after her discharge, she was skipping meals again. But by bolstering everything she had absorbed during her inpatient treatment with weekly therapy sessions, Kathy, who now weighs 123 pounds, has managed to keep her disorder in check.

Kathy and Janice Worry About Their Children

Even so, Kathy still faces challenges. At her daughter's soccer matches, for instance, "all the mothers bring so much food." The sight of so many treats still has the power to send Kathy into a tailspin. When she gets stressed out, she forces herself to take time out for herself: "I'll go for a walk or I'll be by myself for a little while—just enough to get my head straight and tell myself that if I'm going to be there for my family, I need to focus on what's best for me." When she returns from her walks, she always finds herself feeling better. . . .

Luckily Kathy [and] Janice . . . escaped with no long-term health problems. But their one lingering concern is the effect their ordeals might have on their children. Since eating disorders are strongly hereditary and are triggered by environmental factors—like the example set by one's own mother—these women have good reason to worry. Unfortunately, in Janice's case, the worst-case scenario has already happened: Her 15-

year-old daughter is anorexic. Shortly after Janice emerged
from inpatient therapy, her five-foot-six daughter starved herself down to 100 pounds. "She was lying, hiding her food. It
was a fight to get her to eat dinner," Janice says. "It felt all too
familiar." Her daughter is now in recovery, following intensive
treatment, and mother and daughter are concentrating on seeing each other through it. "I tell myself that there's no point in
blaming myself," she says. "But it's hard."

While . . . these women may always be haunted by their
disorders, they are hopeful that the worst is behind them.

7
Athletes Are More Vulnerable to Anorexia than Nonathletes

Lynette Lamb

Lynette Lamb is a freelance writer and editor of Daughters, *a magazine for parents of girls.*

Girls who are involved in athletics are at greater risk of developing anorexia than those who do not participate in organized sports. Further, sports that involve individual judging—such as gymnastics, ice skating, and diving—or endurance—such as running and swimming—cause girls to be most vulnerable to eating disorders. One of the factors contributing to the high rate of eating disorders among young female athletes is that male coaches often transfer their knowledge of male athletes to female athletes and demand that they maintain excessively low body fat percentages. Parents of girls involved in sports should be vigilant and talk to their daughters and their daughters' coaches at the first sign of an eating disorder.

Mom: "I wish you'd eat more dinner."

Daughter: "I ate plenty. Besides, fat runners lose races."

Mom: "You're hardly fat. And don't athletes need calories for energy?"

Daughter: "The leaner I am, the better time I'll make. Just watch!"

Participating in sports certainly gives your daughter exercise and confidence and teaches her about teamwork. However, athletic involvement is no panacea. No matter how active your daughter is, no matter how seriously involved in her sport, she could still be worried about her weight and could still be dieting. And that may put her at risk for an eating disorder.

In fact, if she's an athlete in certain sports, such as gymnastics or track, she is more likely than the average girl to have an eating disorder. Eating disorders (ED) are on the rise among female athletes, says Mary Jo Kane, director of the Tucker Center for Research on Girls and Women in Sport. "An alarming number of female athletes and their coaches have bought into the notion that 'thin wins.'"

A Serious Problem

Just how significant is the problem of eating disorders among female athletes? Try this out for size: Thirteen percent of female athletes suffer from eating disorders versus just 3 percent of the general female population. That's what eating disorder specialist Dr. Craig Johnson (with Laureate Psychiatric Clinic in Tulsa, Oklahoma) and his colleagues found in a recent study of female athletes at 11 NCAA Division I schools.

And even that alarmingly high rate is what Johnson calls a conservative estimate. Despite a large sample and rigorous methodology, the study was slightly flawed because the NCAA banned follow-up calls by the researchers. All of which has left Johnson and his colleagues believing that eating disorder rates among college female athletes might be higher than their study showed.

An additional 16 percent of respondents reported a drive for thinness comparable to eating disorder patients, he says. And 19 percent of the total group reported a level of body dissatisfaction comparable to ED patients, Johnson says.

Certain Sports Are Riskier

Unsurprisingly, sports are not created equal when it comes to eating disorder risk. The highest risk sports are ones based on judging—gymnastics, ice skating, and diving—or endurance—track/cross-country and swimming.

What is it about these particular sports that puts girls at greater risk? In the judged sports, says Johnson, girls compete in scanty or tight-fitting clothing and are thus concerned about "appearance thinness." They know from experience that judges, influenced by popular culture, tend to reward thinness, independent of a girl's skill in the sport. The gymnastics community, which has seen many ED victims and at least one well-publicized death (that of U.S. gymnast Christy Henrich), has been particularly at fault, says Johnson. He adds, however, that it has begun addressing this issue lately, with gymnasts' weights going up again.

In endurance sports like running, athletes are more concerned with "performance thinness"—the belief that the lower their percentage of body fat, the better their performance will be. While that is often true for male endurance athletes, it's a dangerous idea for women and girls, Johnson says.

Women and girls need at least 17 percent body fat to menstruate, and 22 to 25 percent body fat for normal fertility. Combine dieting with a training regimen, and girl athletes often stop menstruating (a condition known as amenorrhea). Amenorrhea contributes to an obsession with food, leading to a vicious—and often deadly—cycle.

One of the scariest things about dieting, says Johnson, is that a subgroup of people seems to have a genetic liability related to weight loss. When the weight of those people drops too low, it triggers a compulsion to diet that takes on a life of its own—almost like alcoholism. "It's a chemical crapshoot," he says.

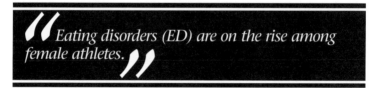

Eating disorders (ED) are on the rise among female athletes.

Despite these hazards, the NCAA survey found that fully 70 percent of female athletes aspired to get their body fat lower than the dangerous 17 percent threshold. "It's male coaches trying to transfer their knowledge of male athletes and performance onto female athletes." Training girls in a method that equates low body fat with peak performance can bring disastrous results, Johnson says. "All of us need to understand the risk of weight loss and realize that girls' weight loss is not a benign behavior."

Anorexia Can Be Deadly

In fact, eating disorders are often deadly. University of Minnesota psychiatrist and eating disorder specialist Dr. Scott Crow says ED have the second highest death rates of any mental illness (only opium addicts have a higher one), and the highest suicide rates. In a 10-year study of anorexics, Crow found that 10 percent had died of their disease, either from suicide or from medical complications like heart failure.

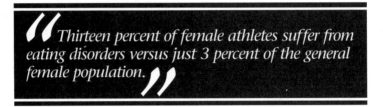

Thirteen percent of female athletes suffer from eating disorders versus just 3 percent of the general female population.

Even if a daughter recovers from an eating disorder, her bones and major organs may not. Young women with eating disorders are at a higher risk for osteoporosis, infertility, and heart problems. Recovered victims often never make up for the bone loss or heart damage they have suffered, and frequently cannot bear children.

Self-Esteem Is Important

For all these reasons, Johnson has this advice for parents: "If your girl says she wants to lose weight, you should approach that with the same seriousness that you would approach her saying that she wants to have cosmetic surgery or to use birth control pills." Treating dieting as a trivial matter has helped lead to our culture's alarming rise in eating disorders, he says.

If you suspect a problem with your athlete-daughter, speak to her about it right away with concern but without confrontation, and then talk to her coach. Parents and coaches need to work together to help girls with eating disorders, emphasizes former college track coach Vanessa Seljeskog. Although coaches are not eating disorder experts, they can be key parental and therapeutic allies, but only if they are educated about ED, she says. Meanwhile, forcing your girl out of her sport may not be a good approach unless her health is in immediate danger, Seljeskog adds.

As for how parents can help prevent ED in their daughter-athletes in the first place, improving her self-esteem seems to be key. Johnson's NCAA study showed that black female athletes, who had much lower rates of eating disorders, also scored far higher on self-esteem measures than did white female athletes.

A girl's self-esteem benefits if it is not entirely dependent on her sport. Former collegiate track star and recovered anorexic JoAnna Deeter cautions, "Running defined me totally; it was all I had."

Ten Ways Parents Can Help Prevent Anorexia

1. Maintain positive, healthy attitudes and behaviors toward your own body. Your daughter is learning from the things you say and do.

2. Avoid conveying a weightist attitude that says, in effect, "I will like you more if you lose weight." Stop reinforcing the idea that fat is "bad" and thin is "good."

3. Avoid categorizing foods into good/safe/low-fat and bad/dangerous/high-fat. Be a good role model in regard to sensible eating, exercise, and self-acceptance.

4. Don't avoid activities such as swimming simply because they call attention to your weight and shape. Don't choose or avoid certain clothes for the same reason.

5. Exercise for the joy of feeling your body move, not to purge fat from it.

6. Teach your girl to take people seriously for what they say, feel, and do, not for how slender or well put-together they appear.

7. Help her appreciate and resist the ways in which the media distort the true diversity of human body types and imply that a slender body means power, excitement, popularity, or perfection.

8. Educate your daughter about various forms of prejudice, including weightism, and help her understand her responsibility to prevent it.

9. Encourage your daughter to be active and enjoy what her body can do and feel like. Don't limit her calories unless a doctor requests you do so for a medical problem.

10. Promote her self-esteem in intellectual, athletic, and social endeavors. A well-rounded sense of self and solid self-esteem are the best antidotes to dieting and disordered eating.

8

Anorexia Is Becoming a Problem in Asia

Jessi Hempel

Jessi Hempel is a freelance writer based in Hong Kong.

Once thought to be an exclusively Western disorder that affected only white middle- and upper-class women, anorexia is now being diagnosed with increasing frequency throughout the world, especially in Asia. In Singapore and Tokyo, doctors are diagnosing eating disorders in as many as one in thirty-six people—the majority of whom are women. Some health professionals blame Asia's growing weight-loss industry for the increasing number of anorexic women. However, others maintain that the weight-loss industry is a by-product of the pervasive modernization and Westernization that is sweeping across Asia. Looking to modern, western women as guides, Asian women have begun to embrace a slimmer body type.

Shortly after Brenda, 20, did poorly on her final exams, she became obsessed with food and began to diet.

"I felt bad about myself because I'd failed," she said, refusing to share her last name out of shame. "I wanted to prove I had discipline."

So she planned out sparse meals each morning, cut out meat entirely, and began exercising for hours daily. When she'd lost 20 pounds—more than a sixth of her body weight—her mother brought her to a new clinic for eating disorders that had just opened at Hong Kong's Prince of Wales Hospital. The clinic's founder, Dr. Sing Lee, diagnosed her with an illness she

60

had never heard of: anorexia nervosa.

Anorexia, a psychiatric disease in which patients starve themselves, was once thought to be a Western disease that affected white middle- and upper-class women. But the demographics of the illness are changing. Eating disorders are being diagnosed in Asian cities from Seoul to Bangkok. In Singapore and Tokyo, the numbers of patients rival the United States, where as many as one in 36 people have eating disorders, according to the National Eating Disorder Association. More than 90 percent of people with eating disorders are women and girls.

In Hong Kong, there are 25 times as many patients with eating disorders as there were 15 years ago, according to Lee. "In the late 1980s, I'd see one or two patients a year on the hospital's psychiatric ward," he said. "Now psych wards see that many in a week."

Until recently, the hospital psychiatric ward is where Hong Kong's patients received treatment once their physical complications became dangerous to their health. People with bulimia, a related eating disorder in which patients consume up to 20,000 calories in one seating, then purge the food through induced vomiting, went undiagnosed and untreated because their symptoms are easier to hide.

"These patients needed a lot of time with the doctor in counseling," Lee said. "The medical system didn't have the capacity to meet their needs."

So two years ago, Lee opened Hong Kong Eating Disorder Clinic, the city's only clinic for patients suffering from anorexia and bulimia. The clinic received 300 phone calls from potential patients during its first week in operation. With a piano, a karaoke machine, and a pile of fashion magazines, its interior looks more like a living room than a clinic in the sterile hospital that houses it. But in Hong Kong, it is the frontline in the battle to confront eating disorders.

A Booming Market for Diet Aids

Many health professionals blame the sudden increase in patients with eating disorders on Hong Kong's ballooning weight-loss industry. Consumers can purchase diarrhea-inducing herbal teas, slimming pills, cellulite creams and products to tone and thin face muscles. And fitness centers are sprouting up on nearly every city block in business districts.

"My friends skip lunch routinely and everyone is on a diet," said Eunice Leung, 24. A long-haired woman in stylish clothes that accentuate a thin frame, Leung attends university during the school year in New York. "It's OK for women to have a little tummy in America. There's more pressure in Hong Kong. Even if you're flat, you want to be even smaller."

But most doctors agree the weight-loss industry is a byproduct of a larger phenomenon in Asia: modernization.

"Asia once embraced many different types of bodies as beautiful," said Kathleen Kwok, a clinical psychologist who works with Lee at the Hong Kong Eating Disorders Clinic. "Because people were poorer, a plump body symbolized wealth and the ability to bear children."

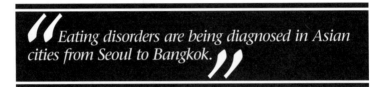

Eating disorders are being diagnosed in Asian cities from Seoul to Bangkok.

A 2000 study conducted through Chinese University compared body image perception in Shenzhen, a city along the China-Hong Kong border, a rural Chinese village in the Hunan Province and Hong Kong. Women in rural China preferred slightly larger body types on average and they dieted less despite being slightly heavier. Hong Kong women weighed less, dieted more and strove to be thinner. The study concluded that modernization equates success with "young, slender, more glamorous women."

Brenda agrees that modern pressures caused her to develop anorexia. "It wasn't my weight ultimately," she said. "I was stressed out and I needed to control something in my life." After two years of weekly 45-minute counseling sessions with Kwok, she considers herself to be recovered. She has been accepted to a university and says she no longer obsesses about food.

"I was lucky because my mother was a nurse," Brenda said. "She knew to bring me to the clinic."

Western Therapy Clashes with Asian Expectations

But other Asian families have trouble embracing the Western style of therapy used to treat eating disorders, Lee says. "The mother—or even father—often wants to know what happens in therapy or they ask the therapist to say or do something to their daughter," he said. "However, from a Western perspective, the therapist is accountable to the client, not parents, in terms of confidentiality."

Kwok said one mother called every time her daughter came in and asked how much weight the daughter had gained. "She got upset when I wouldn't tell her," Kwok said.

A greater barrier to treatment is the lack of information. Philippa Yu, 28, is a social worker at the Hong Kong Eating Disorder Association, a nonprofit formed last year to provide information and support to families of patients with eating disorders. She said many patients search for information about eating disorders on English-language Internet sites. Last year, the association began a hotline for eating disorders. In the first half of 2002, the hotline has received more calls than in all of 2001. Also, Lee recently published a Chinese-language book on eating disorders that's in its second printing.

As the problem grows, so does the need for better and more treatment. Lee's clinic has treated 350 patients. In the next few years, Lee hopes to expand his clinic in Hong Kong and to work with colleagues to set up similar clinics in Beijing, Shanghai, Guangzhou and Bangkok.

Like Brenda, many patients are recovering and leading normal lives again. But with eating disorders striking as many as 1 in 20 Hong Kong women ages 15 to 24, this clinic barely makes a dent in the need.

9

Anorexics Derive a Sense of Control from Their Behavior

Kyffin Webb

Kyffin Webb is a recovering anorexic.

Like many anorexics, I derived a sense of control over my life by controlling the amount of food and the frequency with which I ate. I used food restriction as a way of coping with the stresses of my life. I began by skipping breakfast and then all meals during my junior year of high school. By spring of that year I was diagnosed with anorexia. Despite being under a doctor's care, I continued to lose weight and was hospitalized a few months later. Although I was aware of the damage anorexia was doing to my body, I refused to give up control over the food I ate—the only control I felt I had over anything in my life. I was ultimately admitted to an eating disorder treatment center and began a healthy eating regimen and learned new skills to deal with the difficulties in my life. I still struggle with anorexia and understand that recovery will take a long time.

Whenever I felt like my life was out of control I turned to the one thing I could control: my food intake.

I started out just skipping breakfast, but I soon began skipping breakfast and lunch. Before I knew it, I was skipping all meals. I would go to school each day, and only chew gum. But even the gum I chewed counted as food, because, after all, each stick had five calories. After school I would go to work until 8 P.M.

When I finally got home in the evenings I would have a plate full of vegetables, and then go to bed. I was constantly thinking of food, and how many calories were in everything I ate, from gum to toothpaste. I allowed myself to have 300 calories a day. Needless to say, my weight began to severely drop and my health began to fade. "But," I thought, "at least I am in control."

At lunch the other kids would tease me, and try to feed me, like I didn't know how.

"C'mon Kyff. One potato chip won't kill you. My God!"

Even my teachers were commenting.

"Well, maybe if you ate you wouldn't be so cold." The Friday before Spring Break my science teacher asked me to stay after class.

In Denial

"Kyffin, are you anorexic?" she asked casually, as if she had rehearsed what she had said to me.

"No," I snapped, "I eat. I just eat healthily." I thought that would be the end of it.

I was planning to have a fun spring break. I was going to Florida with my mom and dad, and we were going to relax and enjoy the bright, southern sunrays for a week. But instead of an eight day trip, it turned into a four day trip.

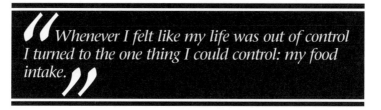

Whenever I felt like my life was out of control I turned to the one thing I could control: my food intake.

It was a beautiful spring night. The weather was perfect. We were eating dinner at an outdoor restaurant overlooking the ocean, when my mother interrupted me to say, "Kyffin, if you don't eat we are going home tomorrow!"

My father chipped in with, "If you don't eat, when we get home, I am taking your car away."

I looked down at my plate of cold and pathetic-looking chicken and started to cry. I buried my face in my napkin, and sobbed. I didn't care if the people around us saw. In frustration I blurted out, "I just can't eat! I have rules about eating, okay?!" The warm ocean breeze now felt icy and I left the table. I walked back to the hotel alone. My parents kept their promises, and the next morning we headed back home. The instant we arrived home, they took me to the doctor, and it was then that I was diagnosed with Anorexia Nervosa.

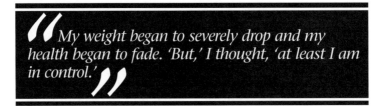

My weight began to severely drop and my health began to fade. 'But,' I thought, 'at least I am in control.'

During the next month, I lost five pounds a week. My weight became so low that I had to be home schooled near the end of my junior year. My body had to eat something in order to survive, so it ate away at my muscle until I had none left. After my muscle, it ate away at whatever it could. I couldn't get up in the morning without every bone in my body aching. I felt dizzy constantly, and could barely walk up stairs. My memory began to fade, and I couldn't concentrate on anything, due to my body's constant hunger. One morning, as I was brushing my teeth, I felt exceptionally dizzy. I waited for the feeling to pass, but it never did. As I turned the corner of the hall, and walked toward the living room, everything suddenly went black. When I regained consciousness I was lying face up on the floor with my mother standing over me. When I heard her scream, "Call 911!" I knew I had fainted. Moments later an ambulance arrived at my house, and I was taken to the hospital. An I.V. was inserted into my forearm vein, and for two gruesome hours I was intravenously fed fluids.

Anorexia Worsens

I was in the hospital when my best friend Stacy gave birth to a beautiful baby girl, named MaKenzie. I spent the entire month of June in the hospital, and when I was finally released I headed straight to another hospital. This time it was to visit. I saw Stacy and MaKenzie two days after she was born. We had both been in and out of hospitals, both our bodies were going through some pretty rough stuff, and we had both lost a part of our cherished teenage freedom.

Stacy was very busy with her newborn over the summer, and we hardly saw each other. But I continued to count on Anorexia to be there with me at all times. Anorexia never told me to eat. With Anorexia's help, I showed no signs of improvement all summer long. My hair began to fall out in clumps, my skin was yellow, my nails turned brittle and cracked, and I was consistently fainting. I lost my hearing in one ear and my monthly periods. My doctor informed me that I would lose all my hair within six months, and if I didn't get my period back, I would lose the ability to have kids. She also warned me that I was at high risk for heart attack. I was slowly dying, but I didn't want to give up the only control I had.

I went to school for two days my senior year and my weight fell. I was taken out of school and placed into another hospital. After two months my weight was still the same. Something major had to be done, and the next step was taken. In the beginning of September I was taken 12 hours away, and placed in an eating disorder hospital in Pennsylvania, called Renfrew.

I just can't eat! I have rules about eating!

At the hospital, my first thought was, "What is the quickest way to get out of here?" The halls smelled like pills and medicine. As I sat and waited for the head nurse to introduce herself, I carefully scanned the hallway. The carpet was an ugly rose color. The white walls were covered with artwork, that said things like, "Love yourself now", "Everyone is unique", and "Celebrate your differences."

What a joke, I thought. As I sat and waited, other girls came up to me smiling and introducing themselves. They all looked genuinely happy, something I hadn't felt in a long time. I wondered how everyone could seem so worry-free in a hospital!

Hospitalization Helps

I spent my first three days at Renfrew crying. I missed my home, my friends, and my old eating ways. But, unlike at home, I received an enormous amount of support from girls who were going through the exact same thing as me. I could finally relate to someone! I began to feel better. I spent the next month in a large house with 40 other women and girls who all shared eating disorders.

Mealtimes were the most difficult times, and there were five meals a day. We all sat in a small dining room and were served our meals. We had counselors watching over our shoulders for the entire meal. We were expected to eat every last drop on our plate. If we left one carrot stick or half of an olive laying on our plate, we were punished in the worst way an Anorexic can think of. We were forced to drink a tall, thick glass of Ensure, a weight-gain drink.

Every day I would wake up at 5:45 A.M. and change into a thin plastic gown. I would head to the nurse's station to be weighed and have my vital signs taken, along with all the other girls. The line was always long, and I'd have to stand in the cold, dark hallway for at least 30 minutes. Once I was weighed and examined I would return to my room and try to fall back to sleep. Yet my dreaded alarm never failed to go off once again at 7:30 A.M. and all 40 of us would then head to the dining room for breakfast. After breakfast we met in groups with names like Coping Skills, Yoga, Expression Art, or Recognizing and Handling Feelings. There I started to learn about new ways to cope with the tough stuff in my life, rather than restricting food.

After group we would return to the dining room for lunch. Then I had more groups until snack time, which was at 3 P.M. After a snack I had free time/visiting time for an hour and a half. Since my parents were 12 hours away and could never visit, I would usually sleep. It was a very depressing time of my day. After my catnap I would head once again to the dining room for supper. After supper I had therapy. Then I would end my day with another snack in the dining hall at 9 P.M. Lights went out at 10 P.M. each night. The days were long, slow and difficult. I missed my home more and more with each passing day. One day, halfway through my stay at Renfrew, the doctor called me into her office. I thought she wanted to check in with me and make sure everything was alright.

Seventy-Year-Old Bones

"Come on in, Kyffin. Have a seat. I am afraid I have some bad news," Dorris warned as she filed through my records. I sat in the overstuffed chair wondering what was wrong. My first thoughts were that something had happened to my parents. It never occurred to me, the bad news had to do with me. She explained to me that I had osteoporosis. "You have the bones of a 70 year old," she told me. "This means absolutely no more caffeine, no playing contact sports, and no more forgetting to take your calcium supplements. Ever. For the rest of your life. Are you listening to me?" I was listening alright, and so was my mom when she was phoned minutes later. This was the worst news yet.

I was slowly dying, but I didn't want to give up the only control I had.

In early October, I was released from Renfrew, and returned home to Kentucky. The first weeks back at home were hard. My grandmother was dying, and since I had been away so long, I really didn't have a social life. My life consisted of numerous doctor visits, which I dreaded terribly. It seemed every doctor wanted to know my weight. That was, and still is, a very sensitive subject for me. I was on my own now. My parents were instructed to let me be in charge of my own recovery. This meant I had to feed myself, and plan my meals by myself. There was no one looking over my shoulder, no one to make sure I was getting enough calories. My weight stopped rising, as my grandmother's health started failing. I started to restrict again, and lost the weight I had gained once out of the hospital. I fell to five pounds less than what I had weighed when I was discharged from Renfrew.

Slow Recovery

I wish I could tell you that I have totally recovered since then, but the truth is that I'm only at the very beginning of a long road to recovery. I am still struggling to stabilize and get my weight up to, at least, what it was when I left Renfrew. I still count every calorie I eat, hide from all mirrors, and refuse to be weighed unless it is absolutely necessary. Every day I struggle to eat enough just to maintain my weight. I feel fat after eating anything, whether it be an apple or a salad.

As I fight to take life back into my own hands, I realize I am going to have to do something very scary. I'm going to have to let go of my best friend, Anorexia. She can never be a part of my life and I won't be able to rely on her for help again, but I know I'm going to be okay. Anorexia was never very good at being a best friend, anyway.

10

Anorexics Lose Control Due to Their Behavior

Lana D'Amico

Lana D'Amico is a former intern at Dance Magazine *and an associate editor at Sterling Macfadden Partnership, publisher of sports, music, and entertainment magazines. She is also a freelance writer for several women's magazines.*

In order to improve my ballet performance and achieve the "ballerina look," I decided I needed to be thinner. I began skipping meals and losing weight. Although my ballet instructor and my parents voiced their concerns, I insisted that restricting my food intake was not hurting me and would help my dancing. After a summer of eating only one meal a day and dancing strenuously, I was showing the physical symptoms of anorexia. Unlike many young women with eating disorders, I did not need professional help to realize that I had lost control of my eating behavior. With my family's help, I was able to slowly begin eating again.

I'm not sure when it started. What I do know is that it wasn't about being thin enough for a guy, or about not being happy in my life, and it certainly wasn't because I thought I was fat. For "real" life, I knew that I was fine. But for ballet, I wasn't quite thin enough, or so I believed.

I'd wanted to be a ballerina for as long as I could remember. While most teens were at the mall, dating, or getting that perfect prom dress, I was at ballet. Ballet class wasn't just something I went to for fun; it was my whole life. When I wasn't at dance, I was watching videos of my favorites, listening to clas-

Lana D'Amico, "Not Thin Enough: When Losing Weight Becomes Losing Control," originally published as "When What You Weigh Becomes Who You Are," from *Co-ed Confessions*. Reproduced by permission of Dorchester Media.

sical music and envisioning choreography, or daydreaming about being onstage.

To this day, I have a hard time saying that I was anorexic. I certainly wasn't bulimic. But while I may not have starved myself completely or binged and purged, I definitely had some serious issues about food. I suppose that anorexia is the closest description to what I put myself through.

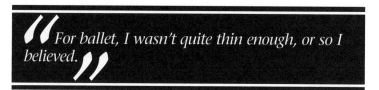

For ballet, I wasn't quite thin enough, or so I believed.

I hear stories about girls whose teachers demand that they get thin, but my ballet teacher, Frank Ohman—a wonderfully talented man who had been a soloist in the New York City Ballet—did not encourage me to lose weight. He actually called my mother once, to ask if I was unwell. "She looked fine before," he told her. "Lana's getting too thin now—and it's happened really fast. I'm concerned." I can't ever recall Mr. Ohman putting anyone down because of their weight. Like a true professional, he was more concerned with ability, potential, and one's level of desire to be there.

Even though my mom got annoyed at me and may have been a little embarrassed about the call, I didn't think too much about it.

Only One Meal a Day

Then, when I was about 17, and deeply focused on a professional career, my once-curvy figure became a thing of the past. My legs were like those of most dancers: a mass of muscles. But the rest of me was skin and bones. My ribcage was completely visible from front to back. My arms looked as though they'd snap, and my face looked way too large for the rest of me.

In 1995, I got accepted to the Richmond Ballet's summer dance program. Faced with competing against talented dancers from all across the country, I was mentally and physically pushed to the limit. I worked hard in Virginia, and cut my intake of food down to one meal a day. I would dance from ten in the morning until six at night; eating only once—sounds insane, right?

That summer, I stopped getting my period. Instead of becoming alarmed, though, I knew it meant I was losing weight. I'd arrived in Virginia at 5'4" and 110 pounds. By the time I left, I weighed a mere 98 pounds.

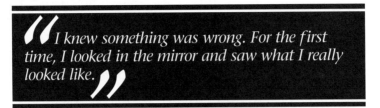

I knew something was wrong. For the first time, I looked in the mirror and saw what I really looked like.

Although I'd learned a lot in my time away, I was eager to come home, see my friends and family, and rest. I can still recall what went through my mind as I took my bow in our final workshop performance—I don't want to dance; I'm tired.

I thought my dancing was stronger, but overall, I was exhausted. When my parents came to get me, they were worried. Through happy tears at seeing me for the first time in a few months, my mom said, "You look terrible."

Slow Recovery

At this point, I knew something was wrong. For the first time, I looked in the mirror and saw what I really looked like. Back at home, my friends said, "What happened to you? Did you not eat a bite the whole summer?"

Not exactly flattering. I wanted to shout, "But you should see how much better I've gotten!"

I knew I had to eat normally and snap out of it. I was tired of hurting my parents and myself. My mother talked of taking me to see a therapist if I didn't get back in a normal eating pattern, I panicked—I didn't want that! So, very slowly, I began to eat a little more, to respond better to my hunger rather than suppressing it. Because I always ate dinner with my parents, they didn't know how little I was eating at other times. I'd be voracious at dinner with them, therefore presenting a seemingly healthy appetite.

Once I started eating properly again—wouldn't you know it? My dancing got better! With more energy, I was better able to attack steps and not be completely beat after classes and rehearsals. When I began to menstruate again, I knew that I was finally back on track. Three months without a menstrual period can be hazardous to one's health, especially for a growing girl.

When I think back, I realize what the problem stemmed from. There's a lot of pressure on young girls. We feel that we need to look a certain way to fit a particular mold. For me, that mold was what I perceived as "the ballerina look." For others, it's something else. Let me say that many ballerinas do not look anorexic. Sure, there are some—but it's nearly impossible to maintain such a low body weight and still have the stamina that ballet demands.

Regaining Control

Instead of shedding a pound or two, I lost control and lost sight of what I really looked like. I was obsessed with being reed-thin, and didn't realize that I'd be too tired to achieve my original goal. It doesn't matter how skinny you look in your costume if you're too tired to dance with the necessary bravura. I consider myself lucky, though. I was able to gain control of my eating before it became even more of a problem for me.

Sometimes I remind myself of what happened. With the pressures of a professional ballet career behind me now, I have to say I feel better in my skin. Oh, I still daydream about what could have been, and I wouldn't take back one minute of practice for anything in the world. I've continued dancing for the pure love of it, and I still adore going to the ballet.

The regimen of dance taught me about concentration, passion, goals, dedication, and plain old hard work. My ballet mentor and I are still good friends, and when I pop into his class he's happy to see that I look healthy. And when my parents get on my case about something, I listen.

11

Poor Body Image Leads to Anorexia

Kathiann M. Kowalski

Kathiann M. Kowalski is a former environmental lawyer who now writes frequently for many youth and teen magazines.

Movie stars and fashion models—obsessed with thinness and often anorexic—become role models for teens with poor body image. Young girls trying to meet the unrealistic standards of beauty and thinness set by the media may become anorexic as well. Instead of encouraging teens to accept healthy bodies of all sizes, the images young people see on television, in the movies, and in magazines pressure them to be thin at any cost.

B rianna slipped quietly out of the house before dawn. She had lost 30 pounds by dieting, but now the weight was creeping back. She decided to try non-stop exercising for three days. Brianna wasn't thinking about missing school or even being alone by herself on the street. She would start walking and just keep going.

Fifteen hours later, Brianna walked into a police station. Her feet ached, and her sweat-pants were covered with burrs from wandering through a park. She was exhausted, scared, and hungry.

A poor body image had led to Brianna's eating disorder and depression. Her grand exercise plan failed, but it had one good outcome. Brianna finally got help dealing with her problem.

Body image is the way you see your body and how you feel about it. People with a healthy body image view themselves realistically and like their physical selves. People with a poor body image feel dissatisfied with their bodies, regardless of whether they are objectively healthy.

Different factors influence a teen's body image. "Certainly the media are setting standards for how girls and boys should look, defining what is beautiful in our culture," says Mimi Nichter. When the University of Arizona professor interviewed girls for her book, *Fat Talk: What Girls and Their Parents Say About Dieting*, most girls chose a "Barbie-doll" look: tall, thin, and large-breasted.

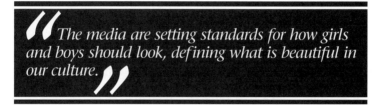

The media are setting standards for how girls and boys should look, defining what is beautiful in our culture.

That same image pervades many ads on television and in magazines. When it comes to males, the media emphasize a tall, lean, muscular look. "People are paid to create an image or an illusion," says Sarah Stinson, head of the eating disorders program at Fairview Red Wing Health Services in Minnesota.

Only about 2 percent of women are as thin as most models, says the National Eating Disorders Association. Models work full-time with exercise trainers, makeup artists, and others to maintain their appearance. At photo shoots, clips and weights mold clothes to flatter a model's body. Once images are shot, computer artists take over. They airbrush pictures to remove any flaws. They can even change the shape of the bodies in the pictures. Thus, the standard media images of beauty often aren't true to life.

Faced with such unrealistic ideals, most teens feel worse about their bodies after reading teen fashion magazines. For those who felt unaccepted or unappreciated in their social environment—up to one-third of girls in one study—the effects lasted longer, according to Eric Stice at the University of Texas at Austin.

"From my perspective," says Stice, "this study is very damning for the mass media." In real life, he adds, most boys think a starved waif look is ugly for girls. And most girls don't like seeing mega-muscles on guys.

Peer pressure also influences a teen's body image. "Teasing

can be very painful," says Nichter. "Kids seem to remember that for a very long time."

Frequent talking about weight can wear down someone's body image too. "I guess I started thinking I was fat at the start of high school," says Brianna. "Girls talk about it all the time at school—who's on diets. I would compare myself to other people, and I guess I thought I was fat."

"The majority of young women feel insecure," says Stinson. "What's happening is they're projecting those insecurities on each other, and you're getting this very competitive environment."

Families factor in too. When Brianna was little, her father sometimes commented on her eating a lot. Her brother sometimes called her a "fat pig." In other families, parents may tell a boy to eat so he grows up "big and strong." Or they may wistfully say that a daughter has "such a pretty face"—implying that the rest of her body is ugly.

Internalizing Negative Messages

Young people internalize those messages. In a study by the Centers for Disease Control and Prevention (CDC), around 30 percent of students thought they were overweight. In reality, less than 14 percent of students were "at risk for becoming overweight." (The term refers to students whose body mass index was above the 85th percentile.)

The standard media images of beauty often aren't true to life.

Yet the 14 percent figure is also a problem. Nearly one-third of students get little or no physical activity, reports the CDC. Higher weight and a sedentary lifestyle increase the risks for diabetes, heart disease, and other health problems. Meanwhile, young people at the higher ranges of the weight scale often feel more frustrated by the gap between what they see in the mirror and what they see in the media.

Puberty complicates things. Girls get taller and gain an average of 25 pounds. They need the added fat for breast development and to enable them to conceive and carry babies as adults.

"Young women don't believe that they should gain fat," says Stinson. "They're terrified of it and don't understand the healthy role of natural body fat in development."

Boys get taller and more muscular as their bodies mature. That's generally consistent with our culture's ideal for males. But not all boys mature at the same rate. And not everyone gains muscle like the images featured in sports and fitness magazines.

When teens have a poor body image, self-esteem dips. Relationships suffer too. Conversations with friends may center on dieting and exercise, to the exclusion of other topics. Teens focus more on how they look than on what they want to accomplish in life. Instead of bonding with each other, teens often become competitive. That fuels feelings of isolation.

In the worst cases, eating disorders and other unhealthy behaviors develop. Eating disorders are more common among females than males. Yet the National Eating Disorders Association says about 10 percent of patients are male. (Besides a poor body image, other factors are often to blame. These include feelings of being out of control and, in some cases, a history of physical or sexual abuse.)

The Effects of Anorexia

Brianna had anorexia nervosa. She did not eat enough to maintain a normal weight for her height. Besides looking very thin, she felt weak and had dizzy spells. Because girls need a certain level of body fat to menstruate, she stopped getting her period regularly. With her immune system weakened, Brianna came down with pneumonia during her sophomore year. Plus, Brianna recalls, "I lost hair. And I was cold all the time."

In addition to these problems, anorexia can cause loss of bone density, dehydration, and downy hair on the skin. When the heart muscle weakens and blood pressure drops too low, fatal heart failure can happen. By experimenting with diet pills, Brianna added to that risk. Even "natural" weight loss products can over-stimulate the heart and cause heart attacks.

Binge eating disorder involves frequent episodes of uncontrolled eating, without regard to physical hunger or fullness. Patients suffer from guilt, shame, or disgust with their behavior. They often gain weight, which adds to any body image problems.

A person with bulimia experiences cycles of binging and purging. Even if a patient's weight stays normal, frequent vomiting causes decaying tooth enamel, swollen glands, a sore throat, and a puffy face. If patients take laxatives, they risk damage to their digestive systems and suffer from nutrient deficiencies.

Exercise bulimia compensates for eating with excessive physical activity. In her junior year of high school, actress Jamie Lynn Sigler exercised every day for hours. Her weight dropped to 90 pounds.

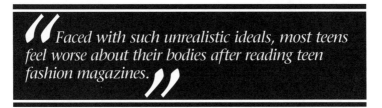

Faced with such unrealistic ideals, most teens feel worse about their bodies after reading teen fashion magazines.

"As time went on, it began to take over my life and interfere with other things that were important to me," Jamie recalled, "like hanging out with my friends, my family, dance and theatre, and even my health." When she began thinking about suicide, Jamie finally confided in her parents. The book *Wise Girl: What I've Learned About Life, Love, and Loss* tells the story of her recovery.

Body dysmorphia, a distorted body image, can also lead to excessive bodybuilding, especially among boys. Some also abuse steroids—drugs that unnaturally mimic the hormone testosterone to spur muscle growth. Risks of steroid abuse include possible outbreaks of violence during use and depression after cycling off the drugs, plus other physical and psychological consequences.

"When you have an eating disorder, you really don't want to talk about it," said Sigler. "You get very defensive. You isolate yourself a lot." If you're concerned about a friend, keep telling that person, "I'm here for you when you're ready to talk about it."

Building a Healthier Body Image

A doctor specializing in eating disorders gave Brianna a thorough check-up and prescribed medicine to help her clinical depression. Brianna also meets regularly with a psychologist, who has given her strategies to build a healthier body image.

"She had me write a list of things I like about myself," says Brianna. "When I start comparing myself to people, I think of one of those things rather than thinking, 'Oh, she looks so good and I look so bad.'" Among other things, Brianna is very intelligent. She is a hard worker. She is great at ballet. She plays the flute beautifully. And she likes her pretty blonde hair and blue eyes.

Dance class can still be a challenge, since the other advanced students are very thin. Brianna is learning to accept that people have different body shapes: ectomorphic, mesomorphic, and endomorphic. Ectomorphic people are very thin. Mesomorphic people are muscular. Endomorphic people tend to carry more fat. Many people's bodies mix these characteristics. Thus, one part of the body may be muscular, while another part may gain fat easily.

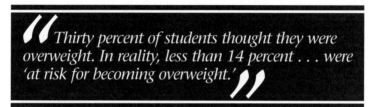

Thirty percent of students thought they were overweight. In reality, less than 14 percent . . . were 'at risk for becoming overweight.'

Brianna also met with a dietitian. When she was constantly dieting, she skipped meals. By nighttime she was so hungry that she might eat half a box of cereal. Now she's eating regular meals and including a reasonable amount of fat. She feels healthier and stronger. Now that she's eating regular meals again, she socializes more with other students at lunchtime too.

Another helpful strategy is to change the pattern of "fat talk" among friends. Sometimes teens join in the talk as a way to fit in. Other times, "I feel fat" can be code for other feelings that young people feel uncomfortable talking about: loneliness, disappointment, anger, insecurity, and so on. If teens encourage each other to talk about what's really bothering them, they can break the cycle of putting their bodies down. Clearer communication also frees teens to help each other deal with problems constructively.

Unrealistic Standards of Beauty

The media emphasize unrealistic standards of beauty. But, says Stinson, "You don't have to buy into these messages." She encourages young people to become activists: Write letters to companies praising ads that show normal teens with different body shapes and sizes. Conversely, send complaints and boycott companies that exploit young people by sexualizing them or glorifying thinness.

Don't fall prey to the dieting industry either.

Even "natural" weight-loss pills can contain stimulants that cause serious health problems. And despite "money-back guarantees," diet gizmos and gimmicks don't work. If any one did work, would Americans continue to spend $40 billion a year on books, diet programs, pills, gadgets, and everything else the dieting industry produces?

You can help educate other young people about having a healthy body image. In Minnesota, teen members of Red Wing GO GIRLS! make frequent presentations to help other young people develop a positive body image. By teaching others, the teens have become role models who are very proud of their own bodies.

Self-Acceptance Is Key

"It's not your weight that determines your health," says Stinson. "It's your lifestyle." Here are some tips for a healthy lifestyle:

• Eat a variety of foods when you're physically hungry. Refer to the U.S. Department of Agriculture's Food Guide Pyramid (www.nal.usda.gov).

• Don't forget the calcium: The Food and Drug Administration (FDA) recommends four servings of calcium-rich foods a day for teens.

• Enjoy regular physical activities. Aim for at least 30 minutes a day most days of the week. Set realistic goals for yourself, and have a good time. The more your body can do, the better you'll feel about it.

Brianna is enjoying dance more now. She also has joined her school's swim team and enjoys the camaraderie with her teammates. When the team members feel tired after a practice, it's a good feeling. "As long as you're healthy and active, and your body is doing everything it's supposed to do, there's nothing wrong with your body shape," she says.

Based on her experience, Brianna adds this message to teens: "You're OK the way you are. Think of the many great things you are—you're like no one else. Just don't ever try to compare yourself with anyone because it's not worth it. You have to be yourself."

12

Anorexia May Have a Biological Basis

Emily Sohn

Science writer Emily Sohn has written for U.S. News & World Report, New Scientist, *and* Science.

Studies of twins provide evidence for a biological basis for eating disorders such as anorexia. Researchers have found that if one identical twin suffers from anorexia, the other twin is much more likely to develop an eating disorder. Studies also find that eating disorders tend to run in families. Scientists have discovered the location of several genes in the human genome that seem to increase the risk of anorexia. Other researchers contend that anorexia can be traced to personality traits that are hardwired into the brain. For example, anorexics are often perfectionists. Acknowledging that eating disorders are real medical illnesses may help those struggling with eating disorders and their families.

Dinnertime was always stressful at the Corbett house. Every evening at 6 o'clock precisely, the five kids would take their assigned places at the table between Mom and Dad. Food was served family style, and whatever you took, you had to eat. You couldn't have dessert until after you had finished everything on your plate. "It was not a relaxing time to sit at the table and eat," recalls Cathie Reinard, 35, about her childhood in Rochester, N.Y. But the rigid rules just added to an underlying tension. As the kids got older, it became clear that most meals would end with Mom's excusing herself, going into the bathroom, and making herself throw up.

Messages about food were inconsistent and confusing to the Corbett kids, especially the three girls. On the one hand, dessert was served every night, and food was always part of family gatherings. On the other hand, the girls, all petite and athletic, were constantly being told they were fat—both by Mom at home and by their gymnastics coach, who wanted his athletes lean. Food was forbidden fruit. Between-meal snacks were prohibited, and the padlock on the kitchen pantry kept little hands away from the candy, Pop-Tarts, and soda stashed inside.

With so many rules and restrictions, it's no wonder that all three girls developed eating disorders, say the Corbetts, now grown and with families of their own. Cathie started sticking her fingers down her throat in high school, after a gymnastics injury prevented her from working out. Her identical twin, Bonnie, developed anorexia in college, dropping 50 pounds off her 5-foot, 120-pound frame in six months. It began, she says, when a boyfriend pointed out her growing beer belly. Their older sister, Liz, 38, was an "exercise bulimic": To make up for eating sprees, she repeatedly pushed her body to the point of injury from daily workouts that could last for three hours or more. Even their brother Daryl, 41, lost his appetite for a few months when he broke up with his first girlfriend in college.

Their mother, Margery Bailey, still feels very guilty about her children's problems. And no wonder. When Bonnie was hospitalized with anorexia at age 19 in 1985, Bailey says the doctors severely restricted her visits. "I was told it was my fault."

Dysfunctional families are still a common target of blame, as is a dysfunctional culture obsessed with thinness. But as doctors learn more about eating disorders, it is becoming clear that genetics and biology may be equally important causal factors for the estimated 5 million to 10 million Americans who struggle with anorexia, bulimia, and binge-eating disorders. Although family and culture may provide the ultimate trigger, it seems increasingly likely that hormones and brain chemicals prime a certain group of people to push themselves to starvation.

A Deadly Disorder

Eating disorders are the deadliest of all psychiatric disorders, killing or contributing to the deaths of thousands every year. An estimated 50,000 people currently suffering from an eating disorder will eventually die as a result of it. Anorexics, who pursue thinness so relentlessly through diet and exercise that they drop to below 85 percent of ideal body weight, often suffer heart attacks, arthritis, osteoporosis, and other health problems. Bulimics eat uncontrollably, then compensate by throwing up, taking laxatives, or exercising obsessively—behaviors that can upset the body's chemical balance enough that it stops working.

As with depression and other serious psychiatric illnesses, eating disorders now appear to be a familial curse. Relatives of eating disorder patients are 7 to 12 times as likely to develop an eating disorder as is the general population, studies show. Depression, anxiety disorders, and other related illnesses also appear more frequently in the same families. That doesn't rule out a shared environment as a contributing factor, says psychologist Michael Strober of the University of California–Los Angeles. But, he adds, "anytime you see a disorder that runs in families, you begin to suspect some hereditary influence."

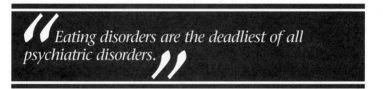

Eating disorders are the deadliest of all psychiatric disorders.

The women in Bailey's family have been fighting a losing battle with food for generations. When Bailey was 18, her 55-pound mother starved herself to death, sneaking laxatives in the hospital until the very end. Other relatives have also suffered from anorexia. "I was always told I was fat and ugly and dumb," recalls Bailey, a 63-year-old retired nurse. She vividly remembers how she and her brothers secreted cans of food because they weren't getting enough to eat at meals. But, she concedes now, the sheer number of eating disorders in her family suggests something deeper going on.

Evidence for Biological Causes

Deadly eating disorders exist in cultures far removed from Hollywood and Madison Avenue and have been around far longer than glossy women's magazines. But if that weren't evidence enough for an underlying biology, the patients themselves are the first to say their eating disorders have a power far greater than peer pressure. Indeed, Stephanie Rose's illness had such a strong "personality" that she named it "Ed." It started with a diet to lose 8 pounds of weight gain after her freshman year of college. But her success became an obsession that landed her in the hospital nine times over the next four years. She crashed a car and a bicycle, both times after passing out from nutrient deprivation. She chugged bottles of poison-control syrup to make herself throw up, even if she had eaten only a bite of a tuna fish sandwich or a few grains of cereal. Even in the hospital, she shoved batteries in her underwear to fool the nurses when they weighed her. Talking and reading took too much energy, so she stared at the TV instead, gray-skinned, too weak to think.

At her sickest, the 5-foot, 5-inch Needham, Mass., resident weighed 75 pounds. She had a mild heart attack at age 21 as a result of her starved state. Doctors told her bluntly that she was going to die, and nurses sat with her 24 hours a day to make sure she didn't pull out her feeding tube. Now 29, fully recovered and happily married with a 15-month-old baby of her own, Rose can't believe she would flirt with death for arms that looked like toothpicks. "It was like someone took over my body," she says, "this guy, Ed."

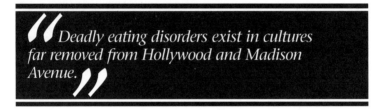

Deadly eating disorders exist in cultures far removed from Hollywood and Madison Avenue.

The most convincing evidence for genetics comes from twins. If one twin has an eating disorder, the other is far more likely to have a similar illness if the twins are identical rather than fraternal. Since identical twins are genetic clones of each other, that is powerful evidence that genes play an important role, says psychiatrist Cynthia Bulik of Virginia Commonwealth University: "Until now, people would have said there wasn't a genetic effect in anorexia. And what we're saying is that there really is, and it's not minimal."

Several groups of researchers are now hunting for the specific genes involved in eating disorders, with some promising leads. The first two comprehensive scans of the human genome have recently turned up hot spots for anorexia-linked genes on several chromosomes, including Chromosome 1, which seems to harbor genes for the most severe form of anorexia. "We now know the location of several genes in the human genome which increase risk for anorexia nervosa," says

University of Pennsylvania psychiatrist Wade Berrettini, a senior author of a study in the March 2002 issue of the *American Journal of Human Genetics*. "Prior to this, we did not." Other preliminary work is pointing to different areas of the genome that may be involved in bulimia, says psychiatrist Walter Kaye of the University of Pittsburgh.

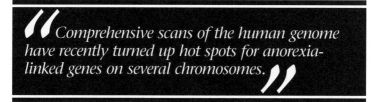

Comprehensive scans of the human genome have recently turned up hot spots for anorexia-linked genes on several chromosomes.

None of the scientists exploring the genome expects to find easy answers or simple genetic switches. Indeed, hundreds of genes are already known to influence appetite and eating regulation in some way, a testament to how complex the eating impulse really is in the grand scheme of human biology.

But some patterns are emerging. The most obvious is that 90 percent of eating disorders occur in girls and women, most often beginning in adolescence. This clue has some experts exploring the genes that control hormone production. During the teen years in most girls, estrogen-producing genes kick in, triggering puberty. And there is evidence, says Michigan State psychologist Kelly Klump, suggesting that those genes may also contribute to eating disorders in some girls: Genes appear to be involved in 17-year-old twins with eating disorders but not in 11-year-old twins, who are mostly prepubescent. But even more striking, Klump says, a study of 11-year-old twins who had gone through puberty and exhibited warning signs of the illness showed the same genetic pattern as the 17-year-olds. Klump notes, by analogy, that depression hits girls twice as hard after puberty as before.

Personality Traits

Other researchers are linking eating disorders to personality traits that are hard-wired into the brain. Anorexics tend to be Type A—anxious, perfectionist, rigid. Those traits can translate into an unhealthy body image: When a driven perfectionist sets her mind on being slender, self-control can become a measure of success. Anorexics also tend to be ritualistic about the food they eat, cutting it into tiny pieces or eating only a specific type of food at only a specific time of day.

Such an obsessive temperament often appears to be inborn. In Kathryn Carvette DeVito's case, the first signs appeared at age 7. She started having panic attacks on the school playground and became preoccupied with getting her homework perfect, starting over and over again if necessary. Then she developed some classic symptoms of obsessive-compulsive disorder: "If I touched a doorknob 15 times, everything would be OK," she says. Kathryn hit puberty earlier than her classmates, and when a doctor told her she was heavier than the average sixth grader, her obsessions turned to food. She dropped to a low of 85 pounds before seeking help when she was 19. Even now, though the 5-foot, 2-inch Boston University senior sees a psychologist weekly and has stabilized her weight at about 100 pounds, she says that she sometimes eats as little as 100 calories a day. She works out every day and does sit-ups in her bed at night.

Brain chemicals may contribute to illnesses such as Kathryn's, says the University of Pittsburgh's Kaye. It may be that people who go on to develop the anxiety and obsessiveness associated with eating disorders have abnormally high levels of serotonin, one of the brain's major chemical messengers for mood, sexual desire, and food intake. Losing weight lowers serotonin, so anorexics may stop eating in a subconscious attempt to lower their uncomfortably high serotonin levels, says psychiatrist Evelyn Attia of the New York State Psychiatric Institute. But when a person stops eating, her brain churns out even more serotonin, Attia says. So, the anorexic gets caught "in a vicious cycle where the behavior tries to compensate for the uncomfortable feeling of biochemical imbalance but can never catch up."

> *Anorexics tend to be Type A—anxious, perfectionist, rigid.*

Kaye also has evidence that the brains of recovered bulimics process serotonin in a way that is different from the brains of healthy people. It's not entirely clear yet if their brains were different before they developed the disease or if dieting caused the changes. Still, such chemical differences suggest that drugs like

Prozac, used to treat depression and compulsive behaviors, might be helpful for treating eating disorders as well. In a small study, Kaye found that Prozac, which helps the brain's pathways work better, helped prevent relapses in recovered anorexics.

A Long Road to Recovery

Despite all these biomedical advances in understanding eating disorders, victims still face a long and uncertain road to recovery. Only about half of anorexics and bulimics ever recover enough to maintain a healthy weight and positive self-image. Thirty percent of anorexics have residual symptoms that persist long into adulthood, and 1 in 10 cases remains chronic and unremitting. Without treatment, up to 20 percent of cases end in premature death.

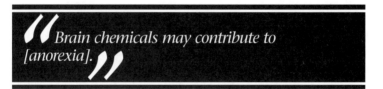

Brain chemicals may contribute to [anorexia].

Denial and resistance to treatment are fierce psychological obstacles once an eating disorder has taken hold, so scientists are looking more and more to prevention. And ironically, given the move away from cultural explanations for the disorders, the best interventions for now may still be psychosocial. Surveys show that 42 percent of children in first through third grade want to be thinner and that 81 percent of 10-year-olds are afraid of being fat. Those attitudes are clearly not genetic, and they are so pervasive that they could be pushing the genetically vulnerable over the edge. "If people never diet," Bulik says, "they might never enter into the higher-risk category for developing eating disorders."

One of the most striking examples of culture's influence comes from Fiji, where a bulky body has always been a beautiful body. Women on the South Pacific island have traditionally complimented one another for gaining weight. Food is starchy, calorie-dense, and plentiful. But when TV came to the island in 1995—with shows like *Melrose Place* and commercials celebrating thinness—the depictions of beauty radically altered Fijians' self-image—especially the girls'. According to a study published in June 2002 by Harvard psychiatrist and anthropologist Anne

Becker, by 1998 the proportion of girls at risk for developing eating disorders more than doubled to 29 percent of the population. The percentage of girls who vomited to lose weight jumped from zero to 11 percent. "We actually talked to girls who explicitly said, 'I want to be thin because I watch TV, and everyone on TV has all those things, and they're thin,'" Becker says. Likewise, non-Western immigrants to the United States are more likely to develop eating disorders than are their relatives in the homeland.

A Costly Disorder

While scientists debate and explore the causes of eating disorders, victims and their families are being hard hit financially. Hospitalization and around-the-clock care to revive a starving patient can cost more than $1,000 a day. Full recovery can take years of therapy, often involving the whole family. But because eating disorders are classified as a mental illness, insurance plans rarely cover the full costs of treatment. Kitty Westin slammed into just that painful wall. Her daughter Anna had struggled with anorexia as a teenager but seemed healthy when she came home to Chaska, Minn., after her sophomore year at the University of Oregon in Eugene. Within months, depression and anxiety again consumed Anna. She couldn't sleep. She withdrew from her family and friends. She stopped eating and spent hours at the gym every day. By summer's end, Anna, who had always been petite, could barely stand without feeling dizzy. At 5 feet, 4 inches, she weighed 82 pounds, and her vital signs were dangerously low. No matter how hard she fought the anorexia, she felt powerless. "It won't leave me alone," she told her mother.

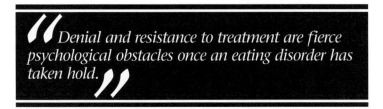

Denial and resistance to treatment are fierce psychological obstacles once an eating disorder has taken hold.

For the next six months, Anna checked in and out of the hospital. She would improve as an inpatient. But as soon as she went home, she'd get sick again, says Kitty Westin, who quit her job as a psychologist to take care of her daughter. The family's health insurance company, Blue Cross and Blue Shield of

Minnesota, refused to fully cover the costs of residential treatment, leaving the family to pay for whatever they could. On Feb. 17, 2000, worn out from her struggle, Anna killed herself. She was 21. Her mother, now a full-time advocate for better insurance coverage, says the family's battles with the insurance company exacerbated Anna's illness. "See, I'm not sick," Anna would say. "The insurance company says I'm not sick."

Real Illnesses

Such attitudes are slowly changing. In June 2001 the state of Minnesota settled a lawsuit against Blue Cross for repeatedly denying coverage to children with mental health problems. The settlement required the company to pay the state $8.2 million for treating families that had been refused coverage. The company is also becoming more accountable to eating disorder patients via an appointed, independent three-member panel that must review mental health appeals soon after receiving them. Westin is convinced that such a process would have saved Anna's life. "There is no doubt in my mind," she says, "that a panel would have reversed the [insurance company's] decision."

A legal acknowledgment that eating disorders are real medical illnesses brings hope to families who already know that their problems won't just go away. The grown Corbett women, for example, all still struggle with body image and health problems related to their eating disorders. Their mother, Margery, was hospitalized recently for dehydration from drinking too much alcohol and not eating enough. Liz sometimes freezes at the thought of going out to parties because she can't figure out what to wear. Cathie, who has a 3-year-old daughter and a 9-month-old son, purged during her second pregnancy and has damaged the enamel surface of her teeth from years of bulimia. Meanwhile, Bonnie continues to struggle with anorexia, 17 years after it began. She takes vitamins and mineral supplements to avoid anemia. She takes birth control pills to keep her hormone levels up. And she has recently started taking medicine to treat end-stage osteoporosis. At 35, she has the bones of an 86-year-old woman and says her hips would probably shatter if she fell. The whole family takes things one day at a time. "You get the cards you're dealt," says younger brother Rick, 31, the only sibling spared by the illness. Instead of cancer or heart disease, he says, his family got eating disorders. "Everyone has their own battles to fight," Bonnie adds. "This is ours."

13

Anorexics Often Resist Treatment

Joel Yeager

Joel Yeager is the editor in chief of Eating Disorders Today, *a newsletter for those recovering from eating disorders and for their families.*

People with anorexia often refuse treatment. Some deny that they have a problem; others are aware of their disorder but are too ashamed to seek help. In certain cases, particularly when dealing with adolescents, doctors might have to to treat a patient even when he or she actively resists. There are psychological as well as legal consequences to treating a patient against his or her will, however, thus most physicians prefer to convince the patient to accept treatment voluntarily. Nevertheless, if a patient's life is in immediate danger, treatment must proceed with or without the patient's consent.

It isn't unusual for people with eating disorders to resist or refuse treatment. As a result, symptoms of anorexia nervosa, bulimia nervosa, or other eating disorders may be present for months or even years before patients feel ready for change. These individuals are usually pressured by family members, friends, or coworkers to seek help, and often do so with reluctance and resentment.

According to Drs. Elliott M. Goldner and C. Laird Birmingham, and Victoria Smye . . . of the University of British Columbia, people struggling with eating disorders may have many reasons for refusing treatment. Some don't think they have an eating disorder at all and feel that their family or friends are exaggerating the problem or are mistaken about the symptoms.

Others may be well aware that they are struggling but are ashamed of their symptoms and afraid of being discovered. Many fear the potential effects of treatment, such as weight gain or interference with their drive to exercise, restrict food intake, purge, or lose weight.

Patients at Risk

In some cases, physicians must consider imposing treatment even when the patient actively resists. Individuals who may be at increased risk include: (1) young patients who have recently developed symptoms; (2) patients who are in immediate danger because of medical consequences of the illness or the risk of suicide; and (3) those with rapidly increasing symptoms.

When physicians decide to "order" treatment, they fully believe that treatment will be beneficial. Many patients in these situations are likely to benefit even if they don't recognize or support the plan.

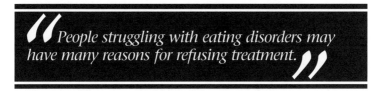

People struggling with eating disorders may have many reasons for refusing treatment.

When treatment is imposed against a person's wishes, the consequences may be great. Thus, physicians carefully weigh the potential benefits versus any risks before beginning. Sometimes, physical and chemical restraints are used, along with tube feeding and restriction of activity. In such settings, patients are often profoundly distressed and as a result avoid further treatment.

Legal Considerations

All jurisdictions have laws upholding the rights of individuals; thus, an individual's right to refuse treatment may be supported by the court. Minors and other individuals who are deemed incompetent (a legal term meaning that a person is mentally incapable of making his own decisions) may be temporarily denied the right to refuse treatment.

While they are competent in all other areas, individuals with eating disorders are often considered incompetent in certain specific areas of their lives, including decisions about their ability to gain weight or their current health and need for treatment. However, patients have a legal right to dispute this, and health-care providers must then turn to the legal system to support the need for imposed treatment. Other health-care providers will be asked to give a second opinion, and to estimate the risks involved if the patient were to have no treatment.

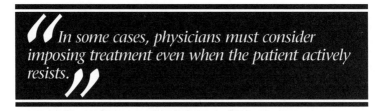

In some cases, physicians must consider imposing treatment even when the patient actively resists.

Depending on the circumstances, individuals with eating disorders may be at risk of a number of life-threatening medical conditions. These conditions call for emergency assessment and response. Although medical professionals can identify an emergency situation in progress, it is hard to detect an impending medical crisis. Given the high rates of suicide in patients with eating disorders, a careful assessment of suicide risk should be undertaken.

Convincing the Patient to Accept Treatment

Because of the many consequences when a patient doesn't want to be treated, and the effects on families as well, health-care professionals often use a careful process in order to convince the patient to be treated before seeking legal means to accomplish this.

1. First, try to engage the patient in a voluntary partnership.

2. Explore the reasons that the patient is resisting treatment. It may be a fear of the unknown or he or she may be frightened by psychiatric or medical interventions in general. Other patients are severely depressed or have cognitive impairment. Most often, refusal to be treated is caused primarily by a cognitive disturbance or such things as a fear of gaining weight.

3. Before starting treatment, some facilities such as Dr. Goldner's use a preliminary intervention. During these sessions, his group provides information to the patients and family members, identifies goals of treatment, introduces staff members,

and talks about specific concerns a patient may have. They also thoroughly explain why a certain treatment is recommended, and what it is. This helps enhance motivation for change.

4. Involving the family in a realistic treatment plan usually improves the effects of therapy. Dr. Goldner's group uses a narrative approach to family interventions that is helpful in defusing family conflicts and lessening resistance to treatment. With narrative therapy, the family is encouraged and supported in developing a personal story, or "narrative" about recovery. This approach lessens power struggles and adapts treatment to the unique qualities and characteristics of each family.

5. Negotiations may be necessary. In order to promote the health and safety of the patient, professionals may need to make changes to the proposed treatment plan. Individuals with eating disorders are much more likely to respond to a professional who is approachable, flexible, and comfortable dealing with conflict.

6. All treatment plans should minimize the use of intrusive interventions, such as involuntary commitment to an inpatient unit, tube feeding or programs of behavior modification. Whenever possible, outpatient programs, day programs, and residential treatment should be used instead of inpatient treatment.

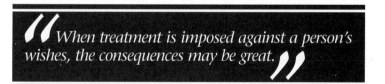

When treatment is imposed against a person's wishes, the consequences may be great.

7. A realistic appraisal of the probable outcome of treatment versus no treatment will help guide the clinician to a rational plan. Imposing treatment should be considered only when the possible benefits outweigh the risks of not intervening.

8. Power struggles between the patient and the health-care team usually worsen symptoms and break down the therapeutic partnership. Patients who feel frightened or trapped may battle staff, have angry outbursts, or withdraw. It is important for health-care professionals to remain respectful and avoid threats or destructive criticism. Treatment should support self-esteem.

9. Due to potential risks, it is generally agreed that legal means of imposing treatment should be reserved for cases in which doing nothing would lead to a serious and immediate danger.

10. Patients who have struggled with eating disorders for a long time often need a different approach than those who have been ill for a shorter time. Chronic illness may indicate a particularly resistant eating disorder and it may be inappropriate to approach treatment of the chronic anorexic patient with a more aggressive plan for intervention.

11. Refusal or resistance to treatment can be viewed as an evolutionary process. Indeed, individuals who refuse treatment at first may later accept it. Usually the gradually increasing recognition of the negative impact of an eating disorder on a person's life is accompanied by a wish to recover. After refeeding has begun, patients may need less treatment due to improvements in emotional and cognitive processes.

Emergency Treatment Is Sometimes Needed

An individual with an eating disorder must be treated, even if she refuses, when any of the following signs and symptoms appear:

- Rapid weight loss, such as more than 15 lbs within 4 weeks
- Seizures
- Organic brain syndrome
- Slow heart rate (bradycardia, or fewer than 40 beats/minute)
- Other irregular heartbeats
- Frequent chest pain on exercise
- Volume depletion
- Painful muscle spasms (tetany)
- Quickly becoming tired while exercising
- Low urine output (less than 400 cc/day)
- Faintness
- Severe electrolyte imbalance

14

Family-Based Treatment Is Effective for Anorexics

James Lock

James Lock is a child and adolescent psychiatrist and assistant professor of child psychiatry at Stanford University School of Medicine. He is also medical director of the Comprehensive Pediatric Care Unit at Lucile Salter Packard Children's Hospital and codirector of the Adolescent Eating Disorder Program.

Studies of the available treatments for anorexia in teens indicate that inpatient treatment in a hospital or eating disorder clinic is likely to result in only short-term improvement. However, a relatively new family-based treatment developed at the Maudsley Hospital in London appears to hold the most promise for long-term recovery for teen sufferers of anorexia. Unlike most traditional therapies, which tend to exclude families from treatment, the Maudsley method emphasizes the importance of the family in refeeding and recovery.

Anorexia nervosa is a serious psychiatric disorder that is estimated to have a prevalence of 0.48 percent among girls ages 15 to 19. Anorexia nervosa combines pathological thoughts and behaviors about food and weight with negative emotions concerning appearance, eating and food. These thoughts, feelings and behaviors lead to changes in body composition and functioning that are the direct result of starvation. As a result, among adolescents the illness severely affects physical, emotional and social development. In addition, there is a fair amount of evidence that suggests that anorexia nervosa often co-occurs with other psychiatric disorders including depression, anxiety disorders, and obsessive-compulsive disorder.

It is not clear what causes anorexia nervosa. The mean age of onset is about 17 and many have suggested that the disorder represents the individual's difficulty negotiating the developmental demands of adolescence. Arthur Crisp's psychobiological perspective suggests that the symptoms of starvation and emaciation are attempts to cope with the demands of adolescence by regressing to an earlier developmental level. Hilda Bruch's psycho-dynamic formulation conceives of the patient as overwhelmed by feelings of ineffectiveness, emptiness and a concomitant inability to access his or her own thoughts, feelings and beliefs.

Anorexia and Adolescence

Recent research supports these ideas in the sense that eating problems initially emerge in response to pubertal change, especially fat accumulation. Other associated risks such as teasing by peers, discomfort in discussing problems with parents, maternal preoccupation with restricting dietary intake and acculturation to the Western values in immigrants also support the idea that adolescence itself is a key aspect of the illness.

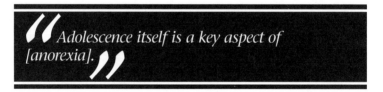

Adolescence itself is a key aspect of [anorexia].

Dieting and weight concerns are part of Western culture. Up to 60 to 70 percent of adolescent girls report such concerns. Therefore, it is important to distinguish between these predictable concerns and those that are more pathological. The DSM-IV [the Diagnostic and Statistical Manual of Mental Disorders] includes two different types of criteria for anorexia nervosa: medical and psychological. The medical criteria are the easiest to identify. Patients who are below 85 percent of ideal body weight (IBW) or who fail to make expected weight gains meet the weight criteria. The DSM also requires that three consecutive menstrual periods be missed in females who have reached menarche.

Psychological criteria include an intense "fear" of weight gain even though underweight and an overestimation of current body mass—usually called body-image distortion. Additionally, it is possible that anorexia nervosa may be complicated by binge-eating or purging behaviors.

Treatment Approaches Are Critical

Treatment of anorexia nervosa requires attention to the possibility of severe medical problems that commonly co-occur with the illness. Changes in growth hormone, hypothalamic hypogonadism, bone marrow hypoplasia, structural abnormalities of the brain, cardiac dysfunction, and gastrointestinal difficulties can occur. In addition, for adolescents there is the potential for significant growth retardation, pubertal delay or interruption, and peak bone mass reduction. Risks of death as a result of complications of anorexia nervosa are estimated at 6 to 15 percent, with half the deaths resulting from suicide. Thus, a therapist working with a patient with anorexia nervosa should ensure that they have adequate medical treatment and monitoring.

As might be expected, patients with anorexia nervosa sometimes require hospitalization. In fact, some data suggests that the total percent of time spent in hospitals by patients with anorexia nervosa is only exceeded by patients with schizophrenia. A variety of investigators have published reports on the effectiveness of inpatient hospitalization for acute treatment of anorexia nervosa. These studies demonstrate that inpatient treatment is likely to result in short-term improvement using a variety of clinical approaches, but because of increasing pressure to reduce the use of the modality due both to its high cost and its disruption of the adolescent's usual life, outpatient alternatives are increasingly stressed.

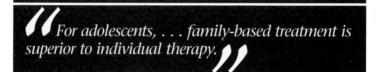

For adolescents, . . . family-based treatment is superior to individual therapy.

There are only eight published outpatient treatment trials for anorexia nervosa. Fewer than 300 patients (or patients and their families) were treated in these controlled trials. Treatment approaches included nutritional advice, family therapy of different types, individual therapy, group therapy and cognitive and behavioral approaches.

The Maudsley Method

However insufficient this data, it appears that for adolescents with anorexia nervosa, a specific form of family therapy developed by Christopher Dare and Ivan Eisler at the Maudsley Hospital in London is the most promising. Studies of the Maudsley method demonstrate that for adolescents, this family-based treatment is superior to individual therapy and that five years after treatment its advantages continue to be evident.

The Maudsley method turns common presumptions about how to treat anorexia nervosa upside down. Historically, many therapists have seen families as pathological and interfering with the adolescent's ability to develop a sense of self. Thus, clinicians have blamed families, excluded them from treatment, and instead focused on the individual relationship of patient and therapist as the incubus for recovery. The focus of these types of treatments are on the conflicts or anxieties about adolescence that anorexia nervosa is helping them to avoid. The hope is that once the patient has an understanding of these problems, the patient will give up self-starvation.

The family is the best context in which to accomplish [re-feeding].

In opposition to this view, the Maudsley method sees a patient in the acute starvation stages of anorexia nervosa as unable to use such insight until after a process of re-feeding has occurred. And perhaps even more importantly, the Maudsley method argues that the family is the best context in which to accomplish this.

The Family Is Not to Blame

The Maudsley method takes an agnostic view of the cause of anorexia nervosa, refusing to blame the family for the illness. Instead, the family is seen as the most important resource at the therapist's disposal. The therapist endeavors to empower them to take on the responsibility for nurturing their desperately ill child back to health. Accomplishing this task requires that the family be able to change its approach to the self-starvation that anorexia nervosa has imposed on their child.

In order to accomplish this arduous task, therapists schooled in the Maudsley method endeavor to place the family in a "therapeutic bind." On one side, the family is warned about the necessity for immediate action to prevent their child from succumbing to the illness—a terrifying thought that leads to increased anxiety, especially on the parent's part. On the other hand, in order to prevent this anxiety from becoming overwhelming, the therapist communicates acceptance, warmth and expertise to support the family.

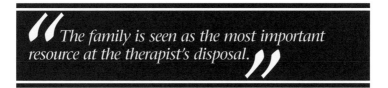

The family is seen as the most important resource at the therapist's disposal.

The Maudsley method owes its major components to a variety of clinicians and researchers. For example, family meals are employed in the treatment and used in a way similar to how [Salvador] Minuchin employed them in his treatment. The process of empowering the family to find their own solutions to their problems is based in the nonauthoritarian stance of Milan systems therapy as well as feminist theory. In order to assist the family in taking on the problems of anorexia nervosa without attacking their child, the Maudsley method emphasizes separating the patient from the illness, a technique based in part on narrative therapy strategies. Nonetheless, Dare's recipe is ultimately his own.

More research needs to be done examining the Maudsley method and it is also evident that clinicians outside of London need to become more familiar with the approach and be exposed to the techniques involved. Christopher Dare is one of the authors of a recently published treatment manual that provides a detailed description of his treatment approach. The manual provides a systematic account of the scientific literature supporting the use of family-based treatment for anorexia nervosa in adolescents and provides specific instructions in the methods used to engage families in this type of treatment. It also includes transcriptions of therapeutic sessions that illustrate how the treatment operates.

There are limitations to family-based treatment for anorexia nervosa ill adolescents. For example, data from the Maudsley studies show that this approach is less effective for older adolescents (over 18) or adults, adolescents who are chronically ill or those who binge and purge. In addition, highly critical families may not respond to the whole family treatment model and need alternative versions of family treatment to succeed.

There is a need to continue to evaluate this and other treatment approaches for anorexia nervosa, but family-based treatment based on the Maudsley model is the most promising treatment now available for helping adolescents with anorexia nervosa.

The Three Phases of the Maudsley Method

The Maudsley method for family-based therapy for adolescent anorexia nervosa has three clearly defined phases.

• In the first phase, the focus is on engaging the family and empowering them to re-feed their child. The therapist reinforces a strong parental alliance around re-feeding their offspring in order to help ensure success. At the same time, wishing not to abandon the adolescent to this process without support, the therapist attempts to align the patient with the sibling sub-system. The therapist directly expresses the view that parents did not cause the illness and compliments them as much as possible on their efforts.

• Phase two begins once the patient accepts the demands of the parents and steady weight gain is evident. The therapist focuses on encouraging the parents to help their child to take more control over eating herself [*sic*] as is appropriate for her age.

• Finally, the third phase begins when the patient is maintaining a stable weight (near 95 percent of his or her ideal) without significant parental supervision. Treatment focuses on the impact anorexia nervosa has had upon establishing a healthy adolescent identity. Then it is possible to review the central issues of adolescence, work toward increased personal autonomy for the adolescent, and more appropriate family boundaries. It should be noted that families have "learned by doing" in this therapy and are often in much better shape as a result of the changes they have made through their re-feeding efforts.

Organizations to Contact

The editors have compiled the following list of organizations concerned with the issues debated in this book. The descriptions are derived from materials provided by the organizations. All have publications or information available for interested readers. The list was compiled on the date of publication of the present volume; the information provided here may change. Be aware that many organizations take several weeks or longer to respond to inquiries, so allow as much time as possible.

Alliance for Eating Awareness
PO Box 13155, North Palm Beach, FL 33408-3155
(561) 841-0900 • fax: (561) 881-0380
e-mail: info@eatingdisorderinfo.org
Web site: www.eatingdisorderinfo.org

The Alliance for Eating Disorders Awareness seeks to establish easily accessible programs across the nation that provide children and young adults with the opportunity to learn about eating disorders and the positive effects of a healthy body image. It also disseminates educational information to parents and caregivers about the warning signs, dangers, and consequences of anorexia, bulimia, and other related disorders.

American Academy of Child and Adolescent Psychiatry (AACAP)
3615 Wisconsin Ave. NW, Washington, DC 20016
(202) 966-7300 • fax: (202) 966-2891
Web site: www.aacap.org

AACAP is a nonprofit organization dedicated to providing parents and families with information regarding developmental, behavioral, and mental disorders that affect children and adolescents. The organization provides national public information through the distribution of the newsletter *Facts for Families* and the monthly *Journal of the American Academy of Child and Adolescent Psychiatry.*

American Psychiatric Association (APA)
1000 Wilson Blvd., Suite 1825, Arlington, VA 22209-3901
(703) 907-7300
e-mail: apa@psych.org • Web site: www.psych.org

APA is an organization of psychiatrists dedicated to studying the nature, treatment, and prevention of mental disorders. It helps create mental health policies, distributes information about psychiatry, and promotes psychiatric research and education. APA publishes the monthly *American Journal of Psychiatry.*

American Psychological Association
750 First St. NE, Washington, DC 20002-4242
(202) 336-5500 • fax: (202) 336-5708
e-mail: public.affairs@apa.org • Web site: www.apa.org

This society of psychologists aims to advance psychology as a science, as a profession, and as a means of promoting human welfare. It produces numerous publications, including the monthly journal *American Psychologist*, the monthly newspaper *APA Monitor*, and the quarterly *Journal of Abnormal Psychology*.

Anna Westin Foundation
112329 Chatfield Ct., Chaska, MN 55318
(952) 361-3051 • fax: (952) 448-4036
e-mail: kitty@annawestinfoundation.org
Web site: www.annawestinfoundation.org

The Anna Westin Foundation is dedicated to the prevention and treatment of eating disorders. The foundation is committed to preventing the loss of life to anorexia nervosa and bulimia, and to raising public awareness of these dangerous illnesses. In addition, the foundation champions the cause of complete health insurance coverage for eating disorder treatment. Information about anorexia and bulimia are available on the Web site.

Anorexia Nervosa and Related Eating Disorders, Inc. (ANRED)
PO Box 5102, Eugene, OR 97405
(503) 344-1144
e-mail: jarinor@rio.com • Web site: www.anred.com

ANRED is a nonprofit organization that provides information about anorexia nervosa, bulimia nervosa, binge eating disorder, compulsive exercising, and other lesser-known food and weight disorders, including details about recovery and prevention. ANRED offers workshops, individual and professional training, as well as local community education. It also produces a monthly newsletter.

Center for the Study of Anorexia and Bulimia (CSAB)
1841 Broadway, 4th Fl., New York, New York 10023
(212) 333-3444 • fax: (212) 333-5444
e-mail: info@csabnyc.org • Web site: www.csabnyc.org

CSAB is a division of the Institute for Contemporary Psychotherapy. It is the oldest nonprofit eating disorder clinic in New York City and is devoted to treating individuals with eating disorders and training the professionals who work with them. CSAB also provides help and counseling for families of eating disordered individuals. Information, reading lists, and links to other resources are available on the CSAB Web site.

Eating Disorder Education Organization (EDEO)
6R20 Edmonton General Hospital
11111 Jesper Ave., Edmonton, AB T5K 0L4 Canada
(780) 944-2864
e-mail: info@edeo.org • Web site: www.edeo.org

The Eating Disorder Education Organization of Edmonton is a non-profit human rights organization celebrating human diversity. EDEO's primary objective is to increase the awareness of eating disorders and their prevalence throughout society. Through education and outreach, the organization encourages people to develop a positive self image based on ability and personality rather than just physical appearance and to understand that weight is not a measure of self-worth. EDEO publishes a monthly online bulletin and provides speakers to schools and organizations.

Eating Disorders Coalition for Research, Policy, and Action (EDC)
611 Pennsylvania Ave. SE, #423, Washington, DC 20003-4303
(202) 543-9570 • fax: (202) 543-9570
e-mail: EDCoalition@aol.com
Web site: www.eatingdisorderscoalition.org

The EDC mission is to advance federal recognition of eating disorders as a public health priority. Their priorities are to increase resources for research, education, prevention, and improved training; promote federal support for improved access to care; and promote initiatives that support the healthy development of children. EDC publishes reports and policy recommendation as well as a monthly online newsletter.

Harvard Eating Disorders Center (HEDC)
WACC 725, 15 Parkman St., Boston, MA 02114
(617) 726-8470
Web site: www.hedc.org

HEDC is a national nonprofit organization dedicated to research and education. It works to expand knowledge about eating disorders and their detection, treatment, and prevention, and promotes the health of everyone at risk of developing a eating disorder. A primary goal for the organization is lobbying for health policy initiatives on behalf of individuals with eating disorders.

National Association of Anorexia Nervosa and Associated Disorders (ANAD)
Box 7, Highland Park, IL 60035
(847) 831-3438 • fax: (847) 433-4632
e-mail: info@anad.org • Web site: www.anad.org

ANAD offers hotline counseling, operates an international network of support groups for people with eating disorders and their families, and provides referrals to health care professionals who treat eating disorders. It produces a quarterly newsletter and information packets and organizes national conferences and local programs. All ANAD services are provided free of charge.

National Eating Disorder Information Centre (NEDIC)
ES 7-421, 200 Elizabeth St., Toronto, ON M5G 2C4 Canada
(416) 340-4156 • fax: (416) 340-4736
e-mail: nedic@uhn.on.ca • Web site: www.nedic.on.ca

NEDIC provides information and resources on eating disorders and weight preoccupation, and it focuses on the sociocultural factors that influence female-health-related behaviors. NEDIC promotes healthy lifestyles and encourages individuals to make informed choices based on accurate information. It publishes a newsletter and a guide for families and friends of eating-disorder sufferers and sponsors Eating Disorders Awareness Week in Canada.

National Eating Disorders Association (NEDA)
603 Stewart St., Suite 803, Seattle, WA 98101
(206) 382-3587 • fax: (206) 829-8501
e-mail: info@nationaleatingdisoders.org
Web site: www.nationaleatingdisorders.org

The National Eating Disorders Association is the largest not-for-profit organization in the United States working to prevent eating disorders and provide treatment referrals to those suffering from anorexia, bulimia, and binge-eating disorders, and those concerned with body image and weight issues. NEDA also provides educational outreach programs and training for schools and universities and sponsors the Puppet Project for Schools and the annual National Eating Disorders Awareness Week. NEDA publishes a prevention curriculum for grades four through six as well as public prevention and awareness information packets, videos, guides, and other materials.

Bibliography

Books

Marlene Boskind-White and William C. White Jr.

Bulimia/Anorexia: The Binge/Purge Cycle and Self-Starvation. New York: W.W. Norton, 2000.

Hilde Bruch

The Golden Cage: The Enigma of Anorexia Nervosa. Cambridge, MA: Harvard University Press, 2001.

Joan Jacobs Brumberg

Fasting Girls: The History of Anorexia Nervosa. New York: Vintage Books, 2000.

Julie M. Clarke and Ann Kirby-Payne

Understanding Weight and Depression. New York: Rosen, 2000.

Julia K. De Pree

Body Story. Athens, OH: Swallow Press/Ohio University Press, 2004.

Kathlyn Gay

Eating Disorders: Anorexia, Bulimia, and Binge Eating. Berkeley Heights, NJ: Enslow, 2003.

Tracey Gold

Room to Grow: An Appetite for Life. Beverly Hills, CA: New Millennium Press, 2003.

Richard A. Gordon

Eating Disorders: Anatomy of a Social Epidemic. Malden, MA: Blackwell, 2000.

Lori Gottlieb

Stick Figure: A Diary of My Former Self. New York: Berkley Books, 2001.

Bonnie B. Graves

Anorexia. Mankato, MN: LifeMatters, 2000.

Tania Heller

Eating Disorders: A Handbook for Teens, Families, and Teachers. Jefferson, NC: McFarland, 2003.

Jennifer Hendricks

Slim to None: A Journey Through the Wasteland of Anorexia Treatment. Chicago: Contemporary Books, 2003.

Marlys C. Johnson

Understanding Exercise Addiction. New York: Rosen, 2000.

Cynthia R. Kalodner

Too Fat or Too Thin? A Reference Guide to Eating Disorders. Westport, CT: Greenwood Press, 2003.

Jim Kirkpatrick and Paul Caldwell

Eating Disorders: Anorexia Nervosa, Bulimia, Binge Eating, and Others. Buffalo, NY: Firefly Books, 2001.

Caroline Knapp

Appetites: Why Women Want. New York: Counterpoint, 2003.

Nancy J. Kolodny

The Beginner's Guide to Eating Disorders Recovery. Carlsbad, CA: Gurze Books, 2004.

Steven Levenkron	*Anatomy of Anorexia.* New York: W.W. Norton, 2000.
Alexander R. Lucas	*Demystifying Anorexia Nervosa: An Optimistic Guide to Understanding and Healing.* New York: Oxford University Press, 2004.
Dawn D. Matthews, ed.	*Eating Disorders Sourcebook: Basic Consumer Information About Eating Disorders Including Information About Anorexia Nervosa.* Detroit: Omnigraphics, 2001.
Morgan Menzie	*Diary of an Anorexic Girl.* Nashville: W, 2003.
Deborah Marcontell Michel	*When Dieting Becomes Dangerous: A Guide to Understanding and Treating Anorexia and Bulimia.* New Haven, CT: Yale University Press, 2003.
Heather Moehn	*Understanding Eating Disorder Support Groups.* New York: Rosen, 2000.
Christie Pettit	*Starving: A Personal Journey Through Anorexia.* Grand Rapids, MI: F.H. Revell, 2003.
Linda M. Rio and Tara M. Rio	*The Anorexia Diaries: A Mother and Daughter's Triumph over Teenage Eating Disorders.* Emmaus, PA: Rodale, 2003.
Tammie Ronen	*In and Out of Anorexia: The Story of the Client, the Therapist, and the Process of Recovery.* London and Philadelphia: Jessica Kingsley, 2001.
Ira M. Sacker	*Dying to Be Thin: Understanding and Defeating Anorexia Nervosa and Bulimia.* New York: Warner Books, 2001.
Debbie Stanley	*Understanding Sports and Eating Disorders.* New York: Rosen, 2000.

Periodicals

Karen Dias	"The Ana Sanctuary: Women's Pro-Anorexia Narratives in Cyberspace," *Journal of International Women's Studies*, April 2003.
Deirdre Dolan	"Learning to Love Anorexia? Pro-Ana Web Sites Flourish," *New York Observer*, July 29, 2004.
Marian Fitzgibbon and Melinda Stolley	"Minority Women: The Untold Story," *NOVA Online*, December 2000. www.pbs.org/wgbh/nova/thin/minorities.html.
Tamsin Ford and Anthony Kessel	"Feeling the Way: Childhood Mental Illness and Consent to Admission and Treatment," *British Journal of Psychiatry*, 2001.
Doug Grow	"Couple Helped Hatch Spar with Blue Cross," *Minneapolis Star Tribune*, June 20, 2001.
Harvard Mental Health Letter	"Anorexia Nervosa, Part II," March 2003.

Bruce Jancin — "Anxiety Disorders, Depression Found in Former Anorexics," *Clinical Psychiatry News*, August 2003.

Journal of the American Dietetic Association — "Position of the American Dietetic Association: Nutrition Intervention in the Treatment of Anorexia Nervosa, Bulimia Nervosa, and Eating Disorders Not Otherwise Specified (EDNOS)," July 2001.

Allan S. Kaplan — "Compulsory Refeeding in Anorexia: Beneficial or Harmful?" *Journal of Addiction and Mental Health*, May/June 2002.

E. Grace Lager and Brian R. McGee — "Hiding the Anorectic: A Rhetorical Analysis of Popular Discourse Concerning Anorexia," *Women's Studies in Communication*, Fall 2003.

Chris MacDonald — "Treatment Resistance in Anorexia Nervosa and the Pervasiveness of Ethics in Clinical Decision Making," *Canadian Journal of Psychiatry*, April 2002.

Jim McCaffree — "Eating Disorders: All in the Family," *Journal of the American Dietetic Association*, June 2001.

Claudia Miller — "Boys Who Binge: Increasing Number in North Bay Vulnerable to Eating Disorders," *San Francisco Chronicle*, December 15, 2000.

Peggy O'Farrell — "Anorexia Increasing, Treatment Shrinking: Families Struggle Against Eating Disorder," *Cincinnati Enquirer*, September 5, 2002.

Terry O'Neill — "Death Wish I: Dying to be Skeletal, *Report Newsmagazine*, January 21, 2002.

Susan Schindehette — "Recipe for Life: A Breakthrough Therapy Brings Hope to Young Girls—and the Families—Who Suffer from Anorexia," *People Weekly*, December 15, 2003.

Carrie Myers Smith — "Eating Disorders and Pregnancy," *IDEA Health and Fitness Source*, May 2000.

Theodore E. Weltzin — "Male Eating Disorders," *EAP Association Exchange*, September/October 2001.

Theodore E. Weltzin — "Unique Inpatient Program Treating Boys with Eating Disorders," *Brown University Child and Adolescent Behavior Letter*, March 2002.

Index

abuse, child, 12
addiction, 12–13
African Americans, 39–44
ALUBA (Asociacion de Lucha Contra Bulimia y Anorexia [Association to Fight Bulimia and Anorexia]), 18
amenorrhea, 57
American Journal of Human Genetics, 85
American Journal of Psychiatry, 40
American Psychological Association (APA), 15
Anatomy of Anorexia (Levenkron), 8
anorexia nervosa
  among African Americans, 39–44
  in Asia, 60–63
  among athletes, 55–59
  average age of onset, 96
  deaths from, 58, 82
  DSM-IV criteria for, 96–97
  effects of, 67, 77
  experience of
    man's account of, 30–38
    women's accounts of, 23–29, 64–69, 70–73
  factor(s) in
    genetics as, 12, 48, 83–85
    personality traits as, 48, 85–87
    poor body image as, 74–80
    self-esteem as, 58–59
  family-based treatment of, 95–100
  forms of, 12
  historical descriptions of, 14
  may have biological basis, 81–89
  among older women, 45–54
  overview of, 10–16
  poor body image leads to, 74–80
  prevalence of, 40, 95
    among males, 77

signs/symptoms of, 11–12, 17–22
  ways for parents to help prevent, 59
anorexic personality, 13
anorexics
  derive sense of control from their behavior, 64–69
  con, 70–73
  often resist treatment, 90–94
  profile of, 21–22
athletes, 55–59
Attia, Evelyn, 86

Bailey, Margery, 82, 83
Becker, Anne, 87–88
Belle, Mabel, 18
Bello, Alicia, 17
Berkowitz, Bob, 8
Berrettini, Wade, 85
Best Little Girl in the World (Levenkron), 8
binge eating/purging, 12
  effects of, 77–78
Birmingham, C. Laird, 90
body image
  definition of, 74–75
  strategies for improving, 78–79
Brooks, Gayle, 40
Bulik, Cynthia, 84
bulimia. *See* binge eating/purging

Carson, Brenda, 44
Carson, Kaelyn, 44
Catherine of Siena, Saint, 15
Centers for Disease Control and Prevention (CDC), 76
child abuse, 12
Clark, Nancy, 28
Crisp, Arthur, 96
Crow, Scott, 57–58
culture
  fasting and, 14–15
  influence of, on eating disorders, 20, 87–88